POCKET KNIVES

Series editor: Frédérique Crestin-Billet
Design: Lélie Carnot
Translated from the French by Josephine Bacon, London
Typesetting and copy-editing by Corinne Orde, London
Originally published as La Folie des Couteaux de Poche
© 2001 Flammarion, Paris
This English-language edition © 2001 Flammarion Inc.

ISBN: 2-08010-550-7
Printed in France

Collectible
POCKET
KNIVES

Dominique Pascal

Flammarion

Are you familiar with the comfortable weight of a penknife deep inside your pocket? This book introduces you to the range of knives available to the collector today, and to some rare specimens only to be found in museums. Although knives are first and foremost tools, many of the examples illustrated in this book are veritable works of art.

CONTENTS

Introduction

The pocket knife or penknife—*mindi* in Somali, *pen-nemes* in Flemish, *soughias* in Greek, *perrochinnii nozik* in Russian—is universal. It is the reliable companion of men—and increasingly of women—from adolescence to death. The knife was born with humankind and was almost certainly the first tool, the first extension of the hand. The first knives were merely chips of very hard stone, such as obsidian or flint, that enabled the first humans to cut, scrape, and even kill—to survive.

Lacking sophisticated techniques, and relying purely on their extraordinary dexterity, esthetic sense, and abilities, Cro-Magnon and other early humans created marvelous tools, examples of which can be seen today in the archeological museums of Paris, London, Berlin, and New York. These stone-cutting tools are displayed alongside bronze knives, of which many examples have survived.

Bronze continued to be used for making knives even after the discovery of iron, because this new metal was not then of sufficient quality for making a good blade. Even bronze knives took a while to catch on, and for centuries, stone and bronze knives co-existed. Bone was also used, but it is an organic material that eventually decomposes, and only a few specimens have survived from prehistoric times. The Lapps continue to this day to make blades of reindeer antlers. Our story begins in the Iron Age, however, since a stone folding knife is something of an improbability. Iron was in general use in Egypt as early as 3000 B.C.E., but not all civilizations developed at the same pace, and it was not until 1400 B.C.E. that it was used in Greece. It took another four hundred years before the Celts discovered it. The oldest folding pocket knife that has been found dates from Roman times.

Early knives consisted of hard stones, sharpened and attached to a wooden handle, held in place by a strip of tendon reinforced with vegetable glue. The examples on the left are modern reproductions made by Ginelli in the Dordogne region of France.

Cutlery in the modern sense dates back to the tenth and eleventh centuries and originated mainly in Germany, France, England, and Scotland. Not much is known about the development of cutlery before the sixteenth century, but it was around this time that guests began to find that the dinner-tables at which they sat were set with a variety of knives, each to be used in turn. A century later, the folding knife began to gain in popularity. There were several reasons for this. As fashion evolved, pockets were sewn into men's clothing; these could accommodate the knives, a novelty for the wealthy. In addition, for obvious reasons, travelers needed to carry their own knives, since they could not be certain of

Magnificent example of a seventeenth-century folding knife. Note the wide, flat bolster and the horn shield covering.

finding any serviceable ones at the inns where they stayed. In any case, country life required a knife for daily use that could serve as a work knife as well as being a cutting implement for food.

The first folding knives, made by the Romans, consisted of a blade and a handle that doubled as a holder, held together by a nail that served as a pivot so that the blade could be stored in a slot in the wood or horn handle. A small round protrusion on the back of the blade acted as a stop, to hold the blade in line with the handle when open. This basic method of construction is still used throughout the world.

Eighteenth-century Spanish sailor's knife. The handle is made of bone, and the wide, intricately worked blade was used for all of the various tasks to be performed on board ship.

Water is the raw material vital for honing any kind of material to sharpness. Wherever there is a source of water in the world, you will find cutlers.

The seventeenth century saw great advances in pocket-knife design, with the invention of the spring. The spring is inserted along the sheath, with a butt-stop attached to keep the blade in place once the knife is opened. This little detail changed many things: above all, the fact that the pocket knife was now much safer to use.

Who has not had the unfortunate experience of having the blade of a pocket knife spring back into the handle as pressure was being applied to it? Fortunately, this does not often result in serious harm. Indeed, it will be shown later that some pocket knives, for instance those designed for children, are deliberately made not to be too good at cutting.

The spring was thus an important development in cutlery manufacture, making knives safer and enabling master craftsmen to produce magnificent examples. The Age of Enlightenment produced the most beautiful knives ever made. Unfortunately, little progress has been made since then.

Grinding-stones were powered by water and were usually kept in a constant state of humidity when the blades were being honed. The photograph shows the interior of a grinding workshop in the early twentieth century.

Every country and each region has produced its own design of pocket knives, creating an extraordinary diversity which should never be standardized. This is a nineteenth-century Spanish hunting knife.

The eighteenth century was a great and glorious age, in which craftsmanship was governed by esthetic considerations. From this time onward, knives were created for specific purposes, such as whittling goose quills for use as pens, "king's foot" knives for measuring, knives for trimming the wick on a tinderbox, etc. There was also plenty of malice aforethought in the shape of a switch-blade, with its hidden mechanisms. Every possible material was used, from the humblest wood or bone to the most opulent gold, silver, ivory, vermeil, ebony, mother-of-pearl, and tortoiseshell.

A certain type of French knife is known as an eustache. It is named for Eustache Dubois, who popularized this simple and elegant implement in the late seventeenth century. The example shown here is in the cutlery museum at Thiers in France. The handle bears the inscription Gabriel Du Naud, J. Delaise, 1739.

Multi-purpose knives, which are now back in fashion, were also invented in the eighteenth century, in an enormous range of materials and shapes. They were not so much "tools" as a "travel kit" of essential accoutrements that included tweezers, a nail file, a corkscrew, long and short blades, an awl, and a pair of scissors. There was even a little ivory spatula to be used for cleaning the ears.

The action of fixing the covering to the handle using a riveting hammer on a miniature anvil has remained unchanged for centuries.

C utlery industries were established in small towns all over the developed world, from Japan to the West. Instead of listing those places in which the art has died out, let us consider those centers where it is still a thriving industry.

The city of Sheffield, in northern England, has been making cutlery without interruption since the year 1000. And what knives they make! The new Millennium Gallery contains some unique examples such as the gigantic, cruciform multi-purpose folding "Year Knife" containing the same number of blades as the year, so one is added annually— 2,001 at the last

The first cutlers always settled beside waterways. This is the place known by the descriptive and no doubt apt name of the "Creux de l'Enfer" (Hell Hollow) in Thiers, the center of French cutlery manufacture.

count. It was started by the firm of Joseph Rodgers in 1822. This firm has been going since 1682, and its military knives are still used all over the world.

There is always a good reason why cutlery workshops are started in a specific location. In the case of Sheffield, coal was mined on the outskirts of the city. In Germany, the one name that springs to mind is Solingen. Here, the cutlery industry is so old that its roots are lost in the mists of time, but it is certain that by 1401 the city had a number of metal-workers who were forging, tempering, and honing steel blades, so the tradition must already have been well-established. Here, too, the location was ideal: Solingen had the river Wupper and its tributaries, which provided the site with the necessary hydroelectric power.

In the past, the biggest market for pocket knives was among country-dwellers and laborers. Their knives were in constant use; they needed to sharpen them frequently and often lost them. Price was therefore a major consideration.

France had several industrial centers that made knives, but only two of them remain—Thiers and Nogent. Cutlery has been made in the little town of Thiers, in the Auvergne region, since the thirteenth century, but the reason why remains a mystery. The explanation could be the river Durolle that supplies hydroelectric power, combined with the extreme poverty of the district. Craft cutlers soon organized themselves into a strict guild. It is precisely because the organization of the guild was so strict in the town of Langres, in the Champagne region, that it lost the cutlery industry that had flourished there since the twelfth century.

This deserted valley, with its relics of the Industrial Revolution, is essential viewing on a trip to Thiers. The Creux de l'Enfer (Hell Hollow) must have been just as terrible a place to work in as the foundries of Sheffield and Solingen.

Many cutlers, some of them master craftsmen, left Langres and its guild in order to escape its constraints. They set up shop a few miles away at Nogent-en-Bassigny, where their descendants still make high-quality cutlery today.

Italy has craft cutlery industries at Brescia, Scarperia, Mondolfo, and Forno Canavese. Toledo is the Spanish capital of the industry, famous for its blades. In Switzerland, the Elsener factory in Ibach was the first to make Victoria, the Swiss army knife, and its successor, Victorinox. The United States has no particular cutlery-making center, but there are many makers of fine cutlery, from those that mass-produce knives by the million to the imaginative, creative crafts-men who produce a few hundred hand-made blades every year.

The strong blade and staghorn handle indicate that this is the sort of knife a French peasant would have used in the first half of the twentieth century. Who knows how many of these utility pocket knives were manufactured?

When all is said and done, a knife that closes or folds is just a blade and handle like a fixed-blade knife, except that unlike the fixed-blade knife, it is articulated. The following is a short glossary of the technical terms used in this book, to help you identify the various parts of a pocket knife. Note that these are the terms used in Sheffield. The terms used in other cutlery centers, even within the same country, may be different.

– **Awl**: a long, pointed spike, generally tri-angular in section, used to pierce through leather.

– **Back of the blade**: the edge opposite the cutting edge. It is some-times beveled, and the bevel is called a swage.

– **Blade**: pocket–knife blades are usually made of carbon steel. The more carbon in the steel, the sharper the blade, but also the more brittle, and vice versa. Stainless steel blades contain at least 13 percent chromium. The latest material for pocket-knife blades is a type of ceramic.

– **Bolster**: this is the part, usually made of metal, brass or bronze, that reinforces the top and bottom of the sheath.

– **Clip**: the part on modern pocket knives that is used to attach them to a pocket or belt. The term is also used for the upper part of the back of the blade.

– **Coverings**: the material that covers the spring and **linings** (q.v.).

– **Cutting edge**: the sharp side of the blade.

– **Damascene work**: the process of combining various types of steel by successive forgings in order to achieve greater technical quality or beauty. There are various types of damascene work, leaved being the most common.

– **Ferrule**: on pivoting pocket knives that do not have a spring, this large broken ring is located on the upper part of the handle and holds the knife in position when it is unfolded.

– **Guard**: a piece of steel, copper, bronze or other material that holds the

hand in place and prevents it slipping down the handle. This safety device is a feature usually found only in fixed-blade (fast-handled) knives. Some guards can be folded.

– **Handle**: the knife-handle that in a pocket knife doubles as a blade-holder. In a fast-handled knife (one that does not fold) the handle is known as the haft.

– **Heel**: the extremity of the blade, hidden by the haft or handle.

– **Kick**: the protrusion on the **tang** (q.v.) blade that comes into contact with the spring. The kick prevents the edge of the blade from coming into direct contact with the spring, which would blunt it. There is a little knick in many knives between the blade and the kick that separates the the blade from the spring in the closed position. This is called the **choil**.

– **Lanyard ring**: the ring or half-ring used to attach a pocket knife to a fob or chain.

– **Lining**: thin sheet of metal placed on each side of the blade, which serves as a handle, or between blades in multi-purpose jack-knives. The outer linings may or may not be overlaid with **coverings** (q.v.).

– **Mark and pile**: these are the two sides of the blade. The mark bears the maker's mark and the pile is the reverse side.

– **Mouche**: this is the name for the top of the spring in certain makes of jack-knife, most commonly those made in Laguiole, France. The *mouche*

protrudes from the spring and also acts to hold the open blade in place. In Laguiole, it is usually in the shape of a bee. It may be forged as part of the back spring or made separately and welded to the spring.

– **Nail**: on crude pocket knives, a nail was used to pivot the blade and was generally

made of steel. In so-called two-nail knives, the second nail is used to
hold the blade open.

– **Nail nick**: the small indenta-
tion on the side of the blade,
which enables the user to pull open
the knife. It comes in a variety of shapes.

– **Notch hollow**: in modern knives, a thumb-rest on the side
of the handle opposite the cutting edge when the knife is closed.

– **Pin**: also called the nail, is the point at which the blade, blades or
accessories are attached to the sheath-handle.

– **Pins**: the rivets that hold the coverings in place and attach them to the
lining.

– **Point**: the tip of the blade.

– **Saw-teeth**: the various indentations
along all or part of the cutting edge
or blade of a knife, making it capa-
ble of sawing as well as cutting.

– **Scale**: each of the broad faces of the handle of a jack-knife or pen-knife. The scales may be covered (see **Coverings**) in bone, ivory, horn, etc., or they may have exposed **linings** (q.v.).

– **Sheath**: a case, usually of leather, in which the knife is kept. It is used to protect the blade on a fast-handled knife, though some pocket knives are kept in sheaths.

– **Shuttle**: oblong shape of many popular pocket knives.

– **Spring**: a piece of steel that runs the length of the handle opposite the slot that contains the blade. Not all folding knives are spring-loaded.

– **Stainless steel**: a type of steel that does not rust or rusts more slowly than the rest. There are various types, including 440, which provides the cutler with a good compromise between hardness and flexibility.

– **Steel**: an alloy of iron and a variable quantity of carbon. When tempered, steel becomes particularly resistant.

– **Tang**: the thicker, bottom part of the blade that rotates against the sheath, above which the blade is ground down to fit.

Lining

N.B. Whether you intend to start a pocket-knife collection or merely want to own one for private use, you will need to keep your knives in good shape. The best way to do this is to clean them meticulously with a cotton bud dipped in warm water. Obviously, you should never subject your precious pocket knife to the depradations of a dishwasher!

The author Henri Vincenot recalled in his book *La Billebaude* how he acquired his first knife as a reward given to boys who graduated from French grade school, a symbol of their entry into manhood. *"As soon as I reached home, I was to receive the supreme accolade, a handsome Swiss knife. This prodigious instrument, which must have changed little since the Iron Age dwellers by Lake Lucerne first fashioned their blades, was seen as a sort of teenage initiation rite in our community…*

My grandfather invested the presentation of this gift with an air of solemnity, for this gift was to become my best and most reliable friend, one that would accompany me everywhere, throughout my life. I would henceforth be using it to cut my bread, meat, cheese, and fruit into little cubes in order to convey them to my mouth, as was the correct etiquette at the time. I would be using it as a tooth-pick, like the grown-ups did, and it would enable me to accomplish such noble tasks as basket-making, carving clogs, or making butter-molds…

Above all, I would be going off to serve my country, France, the queen of nations. I would be cutting a sacred notch on the handle for each month of my military service!"

I

PROTOTYPE

pocket knives

Some people love all types of pocket knife, while others favor a particular style, design, cut, or even a place of origin. Just as some wine buffs only collect champagne or claret, so it is with knives, and collectors will follow the development of the craft over time in a particular center. Laguiole, in south-west France, is considered to be the cradle of the finest cutlers. Opinel, in the Haute Savoie region of the Alps, is another center favored by collectors. One of the most famous American brands is the Buck knife, now made in El Cajon, near San Diego, California.

The firm of Calmels in Laguiole claims to have invented the classic French Laguiole clasp-knife. There is no definite proof of this, but Calmels has certainly been producing clasp-knives of the finest quality since around 1829. The knives reflect various influences. This 1920s Calmels knife, with ivory scales, has a very Spanish look to it.

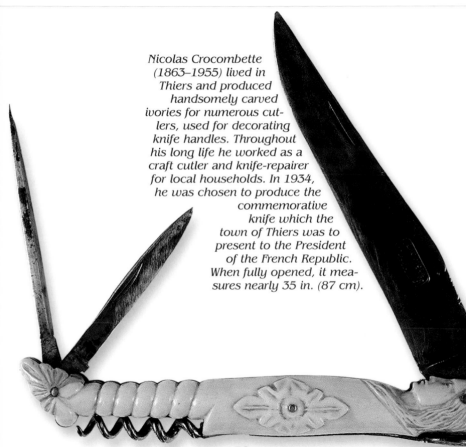

Nicolas Crocombette (1863–1955) lived in Thiers and produced handsomely carved ivories for numerous cutlers, used for decorating knife handles. Throughout his long life he worked as a craft cutler and knife-repairer for local households. In 1934, he was chosen to produce the commemorative knife which the town of Thiers was to present to the President of the French Republic. When fully opened, it measures nearly 35 in. (87 cm).

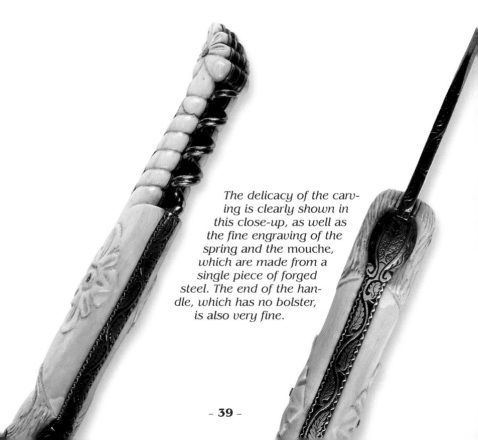

The delicacy of the carving is clearly shown in this close-up, as well as the fine engraving of the spring and the mouche, which are made from a single piece of forged steel. The end of the handle, which has no bolster, is also very fine.

The blades of the three knives on the facing page are made of steel, and the handles of ivory. The top clasp-knife was made by Jules Calmels and dates from the second half of the 1930s. The handle is decorated with alternating triangles of ivory and buffalo horn. The middle knife has a pigeon-wing decoration at mid-handle.

The mouche (a bee in this case) and a chestnut leaf are figured in detail on three superb Laguiole knives made by Calmels, the oldest firm in the town that is still operating. The bottom knife, also a Calmels, was sculpted by Nicolas Crocombette some time around 1935.

These three Laguiole-style knives are said to be "full-handled," meaning that they have no bolsters. They are nicely engineered and clearly marked on the blade. They were produced in Thiers in the 1950s.

These three examples are more modern. The mouche was forged as one piece with the steel spring, the first indication of quality in any self-respecting Laguiole-style clasp-knife. In less well-made pocket knives, the mouches—or bees—are welded to the spring, and thus less robust.

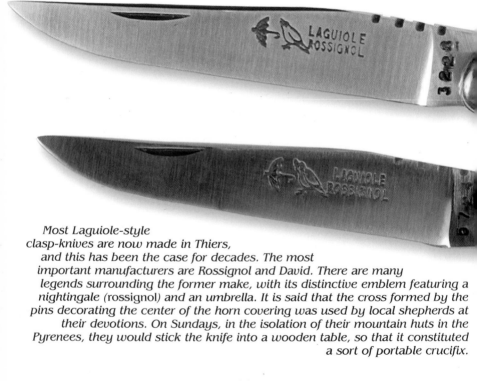

*Most Laguiole-style
clasp-knives are now made in Thiers,
and this has been the case for decades. The most
important manufacturers are Rossignol and David. There are many
legends surrounding the former make, with its distinctive emblem featuring a
nightingale (rossignol) and an umbrella. It is said that the cross formed by the
pins decorating the center of the horn covering was used by local shepherds at
their devotions. On Sundays, in the isolation of their mountain huts in the
Pyrenees, they would stick the knife into a wooden table, so that it constituted
a sort of portable crucifix.*

Le Berger produced Laguiole-style knives
with a distinctive style. The animal heads
which serve as bolsters are in solid silver;
this makes the knives rather heavy
but adds a very aristocratic touch.

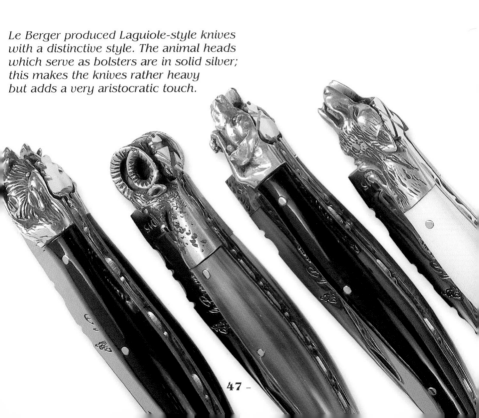

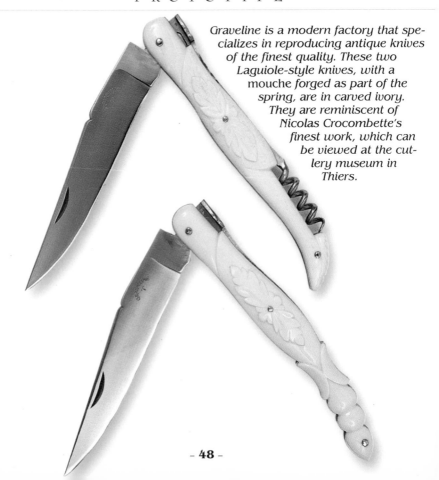

Graveline is a modern factory that specializes in reproducing antique knives of the finest quality. These two Laguiole-style knives, with a mouche forged as part of the spring, are in carved ivory. They are reminiscent of Nicolas Crocombette's finest work, which can be viewed at the cutlery museum in Thiers.

The possible variations on the theme of decoration are infinite. In the great tradition of Laguiole-style clasp-knives, the linings are covered with horn. The region surrounding Laguiole was famous for its horned cattle, so that cutlers had a ready supply of horn "tips" of good quality at their disposal.

This model has a mock-damascened blade and rather heavy bolsters, though these have the advantage of protecting the knife if it is dropped.

Two top-quality products of the Laguiole forges. The first is fitted with a lanyard ring. A range of handle coverings is available.

Various designs have been produced on the ivory coverings of Laguiole knives. One of the most popular is known as "pigeon's wing," carved around the central axis of the covering. This type of knife is known as a crossbow and was made by the firm of David.

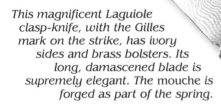

This magnificent Laguiole clasp-knife, with the Gilles mark on the strike, has ivory sides and brass bolsters. Its long, damascened blade is supremely elegant. The mouche *is forged as part of the spring.*

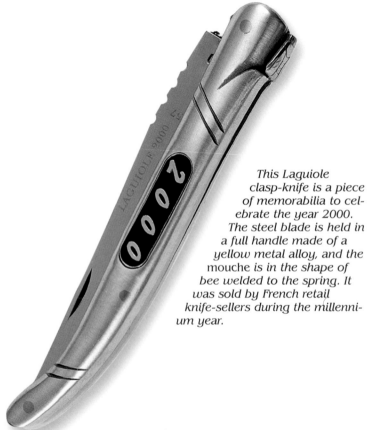

This Laguiole clasp-knife is a piece of memorabilia to celebrate the year 2000. The steel blade is held in a full handle made of a yellow metal alloy, and the mouche is in the shape of bee welded to the spring. It was sold by French retail knife-sellers during the millennium year.

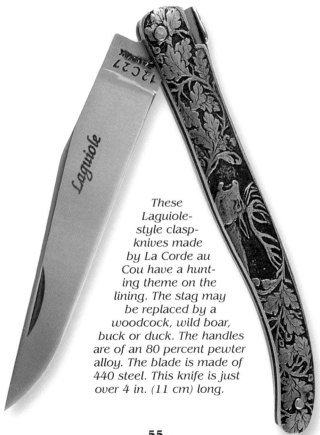

These Laguiole-style clasp-knives made by La Corde au Cou have a hunting theme on the lining. The stag may be replaced by a woodcock, wild boar, buck or duck. The handles are of an 80 percent pewter alloy. The blade is made of 440 steel. This knife is just over 4 in. (11 cm) long.

David is a famous name in the cutlery industry of Thiers. R. David, not to be confused with the firm of G. David, makes these chunky Laguiole-style hunting knives.

The model on the facing page is opened by pump-action. This knife uses a lining lock.

These are two eighteenth-century knives made by cutlers in Paris or Orleans. The blades, bolsters, and pins on these two unusual examples are made of solid gold. The top knife has two blades, one gold, the other steel. The bottom knife has a single gold blade and a delicate pump-action folding mechanism.

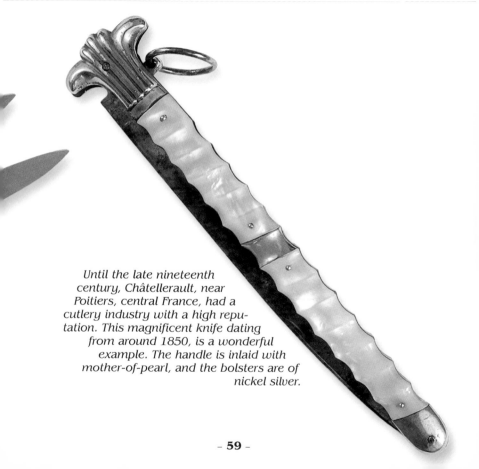

Until the late nineteenth century, Châtellerault, near Poitiers, central France, had a cutlery industry with a high reputation. This magnificent knife dating from around 1850, is a wonderful example. The handle is inlaid with mother-of-pearl, and the bolsters are of nickel silver.

*This etched
blade is typical of
the type of work pro-
duced at Châtellerault.
The whole knife, shown
on the facing page, was
recently copied and re-issued
by Pascal Graveline, a French
artisan-cutler.*

The blade on the facing page belongs to this superb copy of an early nineteenth-century clasp-knife. It was produced in Châtellerault, near Poitiers, on the river Vienne, as is demonstrated by the typical fishtail end on the handle. The bolsters and pins are made of nickel silver.

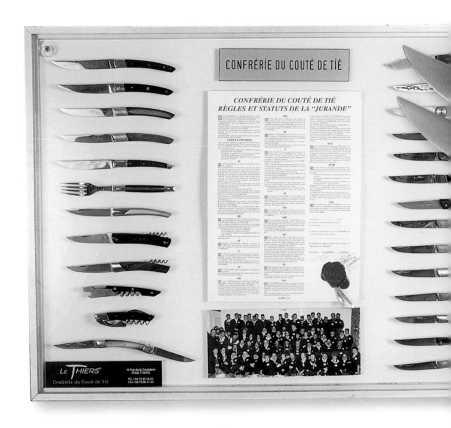

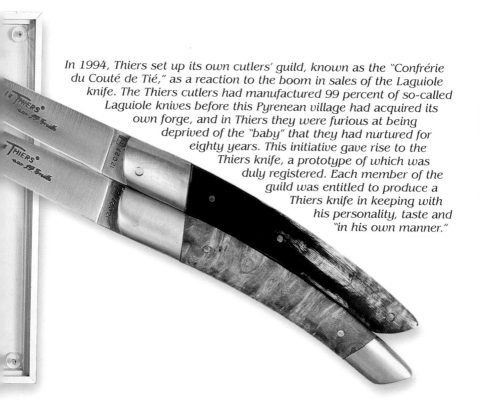

In 1994, Thiers set up its own cutlers' guild, known as the "Confrérie du Couté de Tié," as a reaction to the boom in sales of the Laguiole knife. The Thiers cutlers had manufactured 99 percent of so-called Laguiole knives before this Pyrenean village had acquired its own forge, and in Thiers they were furious at being deprived of the "baby" that they had nurtured for eighty years. This initiative gave rise to the Thiers knife, a prototype of which was duly registered. Each member of the guild was entitled to produce a Thiers knife in keeping with his personality, taste and "in his own manner."

Coursolle is a manu-
facturer well-known for
its inexpensive pocket knives
with brass linings engraved
with figurative designs. There are
several examples on the following
pages. Coursolle is a member of the
Thiers (or Tié) guild. Coursolle designed
this knife combining modernity and tradition.
The linings are brass and are figurative in style.

*Thiers knives
can be produced
using all sorts of
techniques and materials.
This one has a damascened
blade and ivory-covered linings. It
is signed Henri Viallon.*

All types of material are used
as coverings on Thiers knives.
The handle on the left is decorated
with painted vine leaves and grapes.
The pattern on the back of the spring of
the right-hand knife is known as guilloche
and is produced by filing.

At one time, every
European region that
made pocket knives had
its own distinctive style. The
styles known as Corrèze and
Breton (or Breizh Kontell in the
Breton language) are examples of the
revival of this tradition. The Corrèze has a
mouche shaped like a chestnut leaf. The
mouche on the Breizh Kontell is shaped like a stoat
or ermine. Both designs of mouche are forged in one
piece with the spring. Note that in both models, the coverings are held in place by screws rather than pins.

Nontron, in the Périgord region, is one of the cradles of French cutlery, and knives have been made here since the Middle Ages. The area has plenty of hydraulic power to run the machines, and there is also iron ore in the vicinity. The clog-shaped handle is made of turned boxwood, and the steel blade is blocked by a brass ferrule.

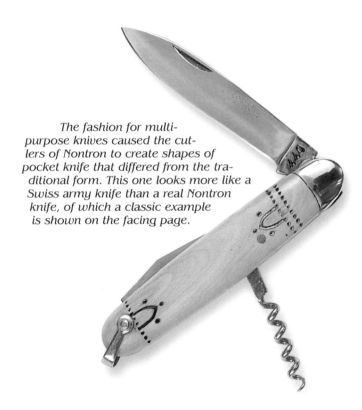

The fashion for multi-purpose knives caused the cutlers of Nontron to create shapes of pocket knife that differed from the traditional form. This one looks more like a Swiss army knife than a real Nontron knife, of which a classic example is shown on the facing page.

This single-bladed Vauzy clasp-knife fits into the spring in a style known as "crossbow." Note the elegant leaf-shaped blade and the long bolster. The linings can be covered in various woods. Here, mimosa wood was used.

The Capucin was sold mainly in the Pyrenees. It owes its name to the shape of its horn handle, which resembles a monk's cowl. Like many other regional knives, this one has been revived by Pierre Cognet.

This Cognet knife design pursues the theme of the Capuchin monk (see preceding page) but this time more figuratively.

*This same design of knife with two pins in
the handle is decorated with a ram's
head in neo-classical style. It is a
perfect reproduction of a knife
once used by shepherds.*

The Douk-Douk
was an inexpensive and
popular brand of knife,
manufactured by the grandfather of current manufacturer
Cognet. The plain handle was made
of folded sheet iron but the blade was
of high-quality carbon steel. The Douk-
Douk was exported in large quantities to
North Africa where it quickly became a
veritable institution.

This flick-knife is a variation on Cognet's Douk-Douk and has a large guard and a scimitar-shaped blade in the Turkish or double Yatagan style. Both the Douk-Douk and this knife are an excellent illustration of how Thiers craftsmen were able to create products aimed specifically at markets further afield.

The Basque Yatagan is a classic example of a regional knife, traditionally made since the early twentieth century—and perhaps even before—that has recently been brought up to date. The knife has a square tang that flicks powerfully on the spring, like the Pradel knife.

Many firms made—or rather assembled—the same knives. This Saint-Amant, that has been made since the 1930s, is a plain single-bladed knife with one pin. It is the work of Philippe Grille of Thiers.

Like most regional knives, the Yssingeaux can be assembled by several different cutlers. The most attractive styles are produced by Fontenille-Pataud. The handle of this model is of mimosa wood.

These Corsican vendetta knives are now made in Thiers, like many other styles that were once the specialty of a particular region. The blades are engraved with various bloodthirsty slogans, such as "May my wound be mortal." These knives, still in production, have blades between 2 and 12 in. (5 and 28 cm) long. These three examples date from the 1960s.

This knife design was especially produced to order by Henri Viallon for Gaumont, the French film production company. The knife was to feature in a television soap opera entitled La Clé des Champs *(Key to the Fields)* about a cutler and the village in which he lived. The series has been forgotten, but the knife, now made by Vialis, continues to flourish.

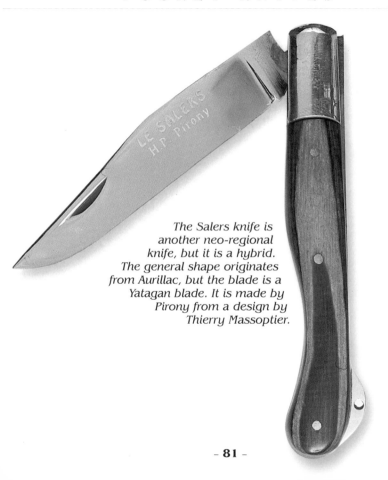

The Salers knife is another neo-regional knife, but it is a hybrid. The general shape originates from Aurillac, but the blade is a Yatagan blade. It is made by Pirony from a design by Thierry Massoptier.

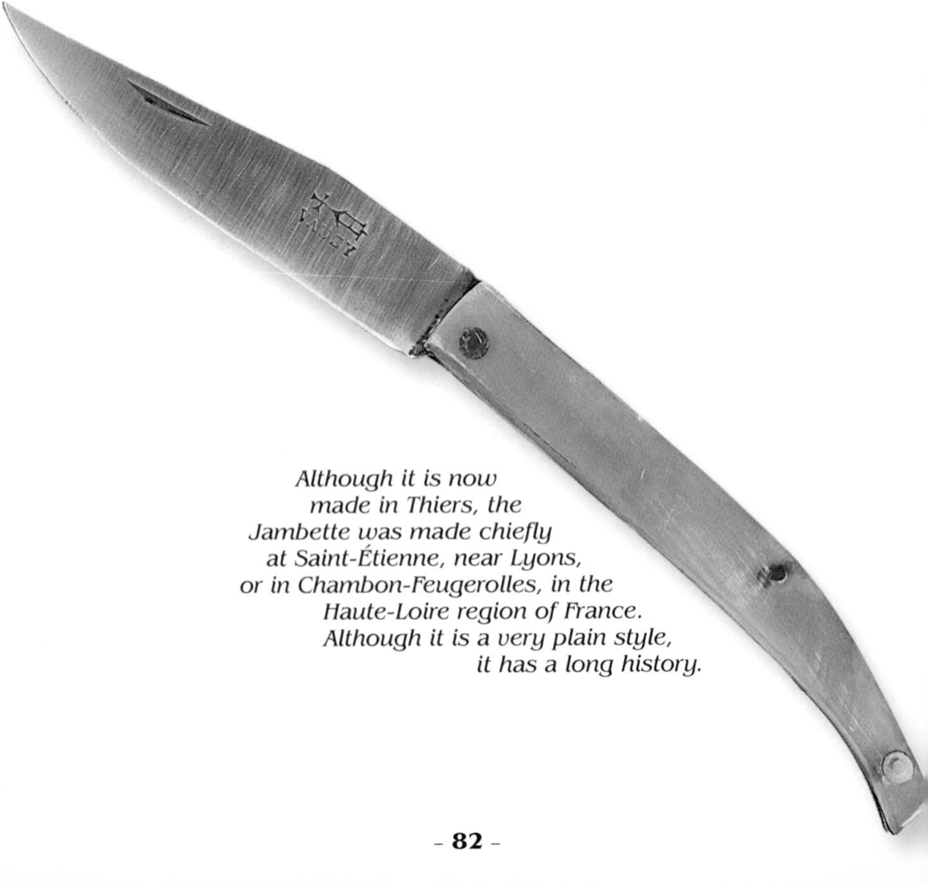

Although it is now
made in Thiers, the
Jambette was made chiefly
at Saint-Étienne, near Lyons,
or in Chambon-Feugerolles, in the
Haute-Loire region of France.
Although it is a very plain style,
it has a long history.

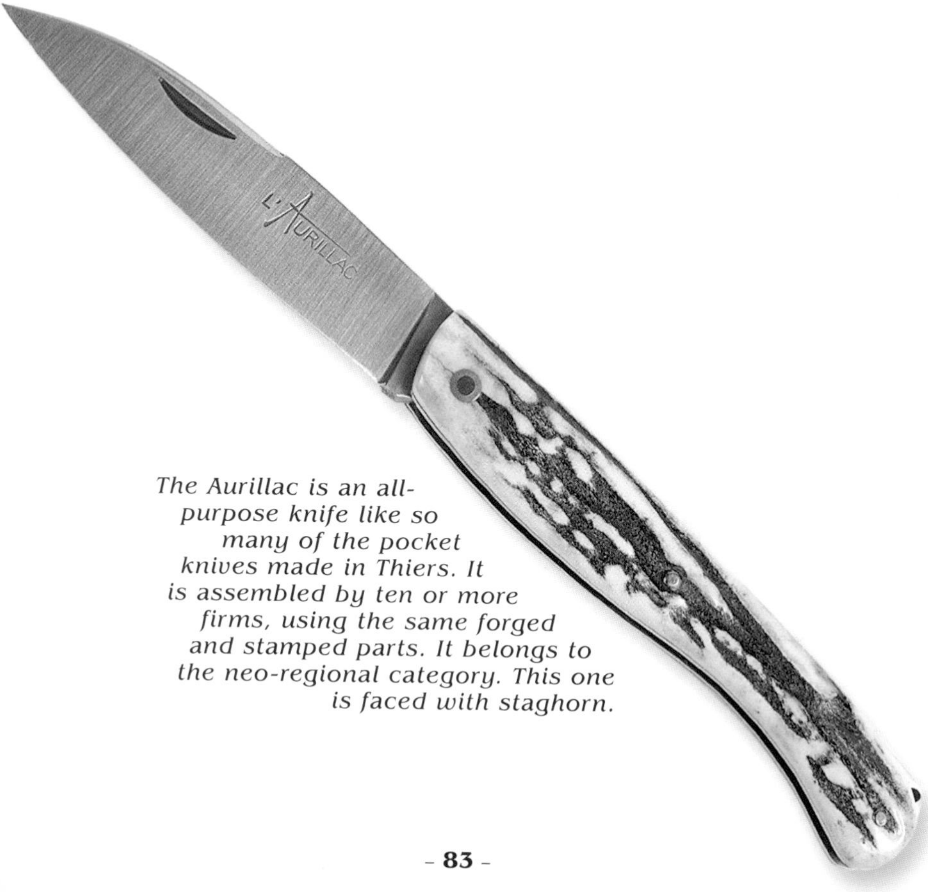

The Aurillac is an all-
purpose knife like so
many of the pocket
knives made in Thiers. It
is assembled by ten or more
firms, using the same forged
and stamped parts. It belongs to
the neo-regional category. This one
is faced with staghorn.

The Montpellier, like the Corsican knife, knives from Rouen and Aurillac, and many others, is one of those regional pocket knives that are once again being made in quantity, mainly for collectors. This Montpellier knife by Cognet is made in the traditional shape, but the materials used are of the finest quality.

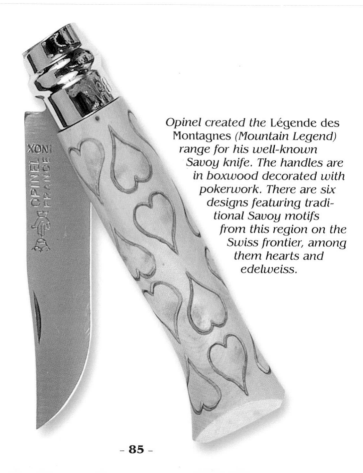

Opinel created the Légende des Montagnes *(Mountain Legend)* range for his well-known Savoy knife. The handles are in boxwood decorated with pokerwork. There are six designs featuring traditional Savoy motifs from this region on the Swiss frontier, among them hearts and edelweiss.

Opinel has extended its range of knives in various directions and has created the Efillé range. These have the typical Opinel handle but with a thinner blade. They are made of satinized or polished stainless steel. The handles are covered in a wide variety of woods, including beechwood, bubinga, cherrywood, elm, olive, walnut, and boxwood. The clasp-knives are sold with blades of 4, 5, 6, and 11 in. (10, 12, 14, and 27 cm). The longest blade makes an excellent fish-filleting knife.

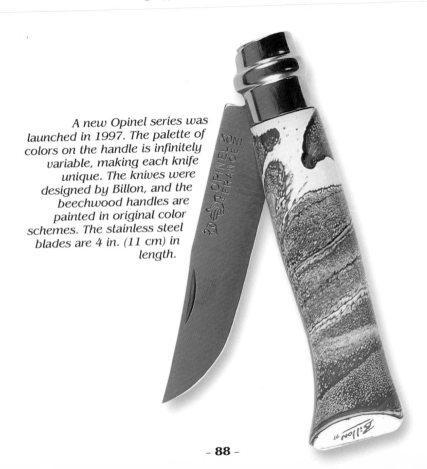

A new Opinel series was launched in 1997. The palette of colors on the handle is infinitely variable, making each knife unique. The knives were designed by Billon, and the beechwood handles are painted in original color schemes. The stainless steel blades are 4 in. (11 cm) in length.

The handle of this Opinel looks as if it were made of carbon fiber, but this is merely the decoration. In fact it is made of ABS plastic. The knife has a stainless steel blade and is finished with a safety ferrule in the distinctive Opinel shape.

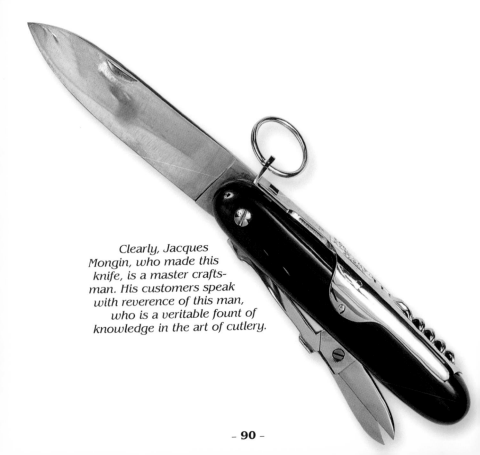

Clearly, Jacques Mongin, who made this knife, is a master craftsman. His customers speak with reverence of this man, who is a veritable fount of knowledge in the art of cutlery.

Three Jacques Mongin models. On the facing page is the Navette (shuttle) model with corkscrew and scissors, and on the right are the Facette and Yatagan models, both covered in blond horn.

To quote Jacques Mongin's advertising slogan, "Nature offers the material, the human hand creates a masterpiece." This very talented craftsman, who is located in Biesles, in the Haute-Marne region of France, makes magnificent jack-knives. This model has an ivory handle and a single stainless steel blade.

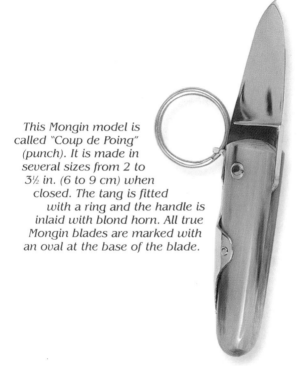

This Mongin model is called "Coup de Poing" (punch). It is made in several sizes from 2 to 3½ in. (6 to 9 cm) when closed. The tang is fitted with a ring and the handle is inlaid with blond horn. All true Mongin blades are marked with an oval at the base of the blade.

All three of these pocket knives have a safety ring-pull catch on the tang. The top knife is branded Okapi and has a bakelite covering. The others were made in Thiers and are covered in nickel silver (center) and horn (bottom). They were made in the 1950s.

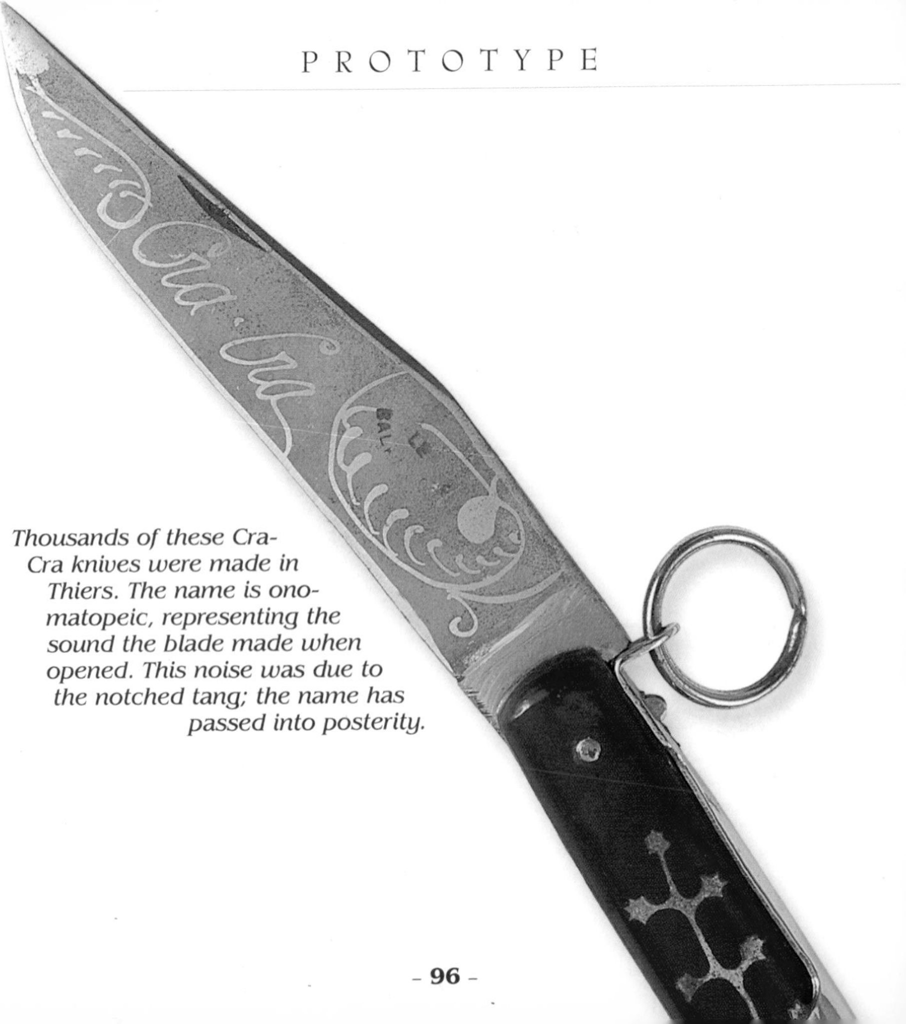

Thousands of these Cra-Cra knives were made in Thiers. The name is ono-matopeic, representing the sound the blade made when opened. This noise was due to the notched tang; the name has passed into posterity.

These switch-blades were made in Albacete, Spain, in the 1950s, mainly for the tourist trade. The handle is covered with horn—allegedly from a bull—and it has steel bolsters and a fob attachment. The blade is splendidly worked.

Two handsome
Spanish navaja
knives. Many pocket
knives of this design
were also made in
Thiers. Spaniards were
banned from carrying the
navaja knife following a riot
that broke out in 1700.
According to author Camille Pagé,
this caused the craftsmanship associated
with these knives to disappear from Spain.

According to the experts, this is an example of one of the finest Catalan knives of the eighteenth century. It has an unusual mouche, and the horn-covered lining is patterned with chips of glass, ivory, and brass. The blade is also superb and in excellent condition.

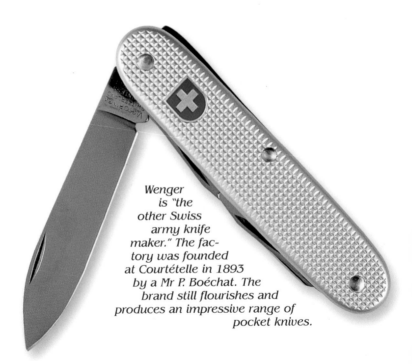

Wenger is "the other Swiss army knife maker." The factory was founded at Courtételle in 1893 by a Mr P. Boéchat. The brand still flourishes and produces an impressive range of pocket knives.

The Victorinox model known as Ecoline has matt, nylon sides on which the logo has been heat-engraved. It is just over 3½ in. (91 mm) long and has twelve standard functions. Note that this particular model has the same livery as the United Nations peacekeeping forces known as the Blue Berets.

This American Uncle Henry pocket knife is typical of the smaller models popularized by Case, Ka-Bar, and Remington. It is actually made by Schrade and has two blades, one of which is very similar in shape to a Laguiole blade. The coverings are plastic, stained to look like staghorn.

This is another Schrade model, this time with a little pair of scissors and a fob attachment. It was designed for use by fly fishermen, who are in constant need of such tools.

American pocket knives were directly inspired by the work being produced in Sheffield, but the influx of German and Italian immigrants also left their mark. One of these blades is shaped like a cut-throat razor, the other is a Yatagan type. It is hard to guess the antecedents of these knives.

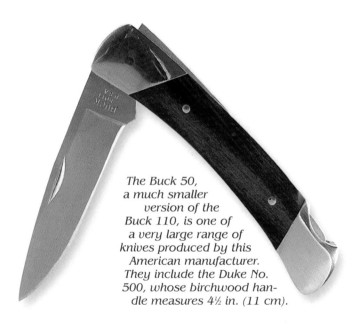

The Buck 50,
a much smaller
version of the
Buck 110, is one of
a very large range of
knives produced by this
American manufacturer.
They include the Duke No.
500, whose birchwood han-
dle measures 4½ in. (11 cm).

This Buck knife can be
opened with one hand, and is
characterized by the milled knob at
the base of the blade and the large
thumb-rest at the top of the handle. This
is the Protégé type. The 4½ in. (11 cm) blade
is partially dentate. It has a removable belt clip
and a pump-action catch.

*The firm of Buck patent-
ed the BuckCote coating for
some of its blades. BuckCote is
a titanium nitrate film that makes
the blade much tougher. This means
that the blade only needs to be honed on
one side. Buck claims that BuckCote gives
the blade amazing cutting power, eight times
greater than that of a conventional knife.*

The Buck 110 is an American legend, created in 1902 and manufactured since then by the million. This is a commemorative model, created for the firm's centenary in 2002. The macassar wood handle is 5 in. (12.5 cm) long. The blade is made of steel, and the bolsters are nickel silver. It comes with its own leather sheath.

This very high-tech looking knife from the German firm of Puma has a straight, stainless steel blade and a plastic handle 11 cm (4½ in) long. Puma has another modern range called Protec, which follows the fashion for saw-toothed blades.

Puma's Economy series (left and facing page) includes the Sergeant with its 4½ in. (11 cm) Yatagan-shaped stainless steel blade, a copy of a Buck knife. There are three other sizes: the three-inch Corporal (7.5 cm), the four-inch Lieutenant (10 cm), and the five-inch Major (12.5 cm).

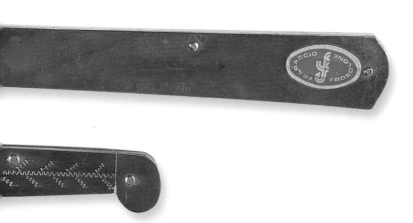

These pocket knives were bought in a market
in Sicily in the 1980s. Although they are very
simple, the blades are of high quality. These
are genuinely traditional knives and are a
worthy souvenir of a vacation.

It would be hard to find lighter pocket knives than these. They are made in China and are sold in their thousands throughout the world. The blades are stainless steel, and the covering is aluminum with a stamped decoration.

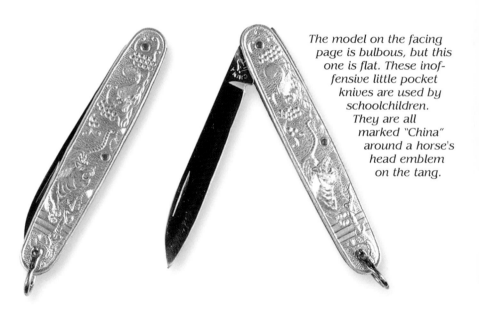

The model on the facing page is bulbous, but this one is flat. These inoffensive little pocket knives are used by schoolchildren. They are all marked "China" around a horse's head emblem on the tang.

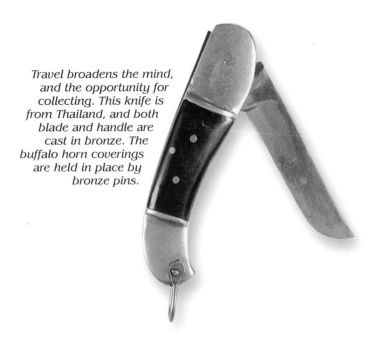

Travel broadens the mind, and the opportunity for collecting. This knife is from Thailand, and both blade and handle are cast in bronze. The buffalo horn coverings are held in place by bronze pins.

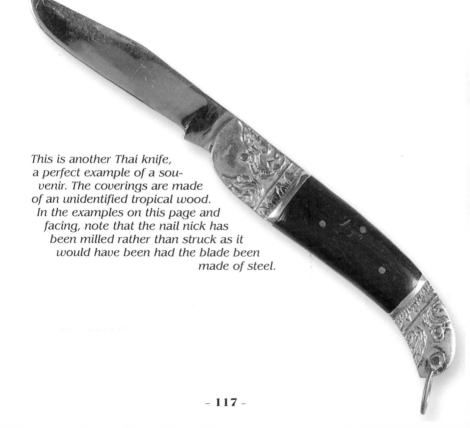

This is another Thai knife, a perfect example of a souvenir. The coverings are made of an unidentified tropical wood. In the examples on this page and facing, note that the nail nick has been milled rather than struck as it would have been had the blade been made of steel.

II

SPECIALTY
pocket knives

The earliest knives were all-purpose, but cutlers soon thought up the idea of making knives for specific purposes. In the eighteenth century, pocket knives began to be produced with specific aims in mind, some practical, others frivolous, and others still that are impossible to guess today.

From this time on, the shepherd would not have the same knife as the notary, the gentleman would not use the gardener's pruning-knife, and the student would not take to school a handsome multi-blade knife in his pencil-case, complete with cigar-cutting attachment!

Two handsome hunting knives with very specific uses. The one on the left is a d'Estaing-type clasp-knife which can be used folded or unfolded. When unfolded, it becomes a hunting dagger, used to despatch a wounded animal. When folded, making it a smaller knife, it is used to carve up the kill.

This clasp-knife curves along its whole length. When open, it measures almost 40 in. (1 m) and is more of a parade knife than a real hunting weapon. But parading also serves a specific purpose...

This is another d'Estaing-style hunting knife (see preceding page). A French admiral named d'Estaing is said to have asked a cutler to make him this type of dual-purpose knife that could be used in two sizes. This is a Florinox with ram's horn coverings.

This knife is for use after
the hunt is over. It is quite
long, with a staghorn handle,
and was probably made in
Châtellerault. It must have looked
quite impressive when placed on the
table at the hunt banquet.

Whenever he visited Paris, Ernest Hemingway would pay a visit to Kindal's on the Avenue de l'Opéra, especially as his good friend Charles Ritz owned a hotel nearby. He bough this knife from Kindal and had the idea of adding a piece o ivory to the end of the handle. At least, that is how the stor goes. Nowadays, Jacques Mongin still makes the knife tha has become known as the Hemingway hunting knife

This is a classic piece of Thiers design, a pocket knife with a single stainless steel blade and pump-action catch. The covering is of staghorn. Issard is almost the only manufacturer of this shape of knife.

*This Mongin
model is known as
the Couronne (crown)
because of the wide base
of the staghorn handle.*

This magnificent
knife comes from
the workshop of
Jacques Mongin. The
damascene blade is forged
by Dourcin. The pattern is
called "Mohammed's ladder."

The most inter-
esting of the old blades
are those that bear the
maker's mark. In this case, it
is Beljambe of Rouen. Knives
made in Rouen often have certain features in common, although this one, with
its shield and mother-of-pearl inlay, is much
more elegant than the formidable-looking peasant knives that also date from the eighteenth
century. The back of the blade has the characteristically
long swage (chamfer). Note the very elegant way the
rounded tang of the blade emerges from the bolster. This knife
can be viewed at the cutlery museum in Thiers.

This attractive knife, whose steel blade is shaped like a cut-throat razor, dates from the French Restoration period (mid-nineteenth century). It is marked Aucoc. The coverings are of ivory, and it has a forged steel corkscrew attachment.

One of the blades on this handsome pocket knife is a cigar cutter, but contrary to what one might expect, the longer blade is the one used for cutting the tobacco leaf. The corkscrew is very well made with a well-spaced coil and centered spike.

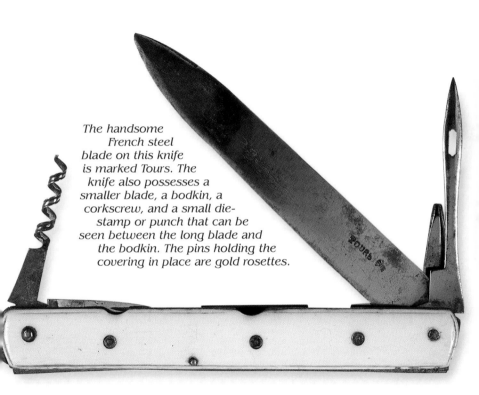

The handsome French steel blade on this knife is marked Tours. The knife also possesses a smaller blade, a bodkin, a corkscrew, and a small die-stamp or punch that can be seen between the long blade and the bodkin. The pins holding the covering in place are gold rosettes.

Here are three handsome specimens of modern knives fitted with a corkscrew, a favorite accessory.
They are all made by Perceval of Thiers. The top knife is covered with bone, the center knife with blond horn, and the bottom knife, the most elegant, with ivory.

*The three Perceval
knives opposite are called
Le Français (The Frenchman).
As for this one, a much older
knife, it is indeed the most typical of
French knives: it has all that is required for a
splendid impromptu picnic—a blade and a
corkscrew. Anything else would be superfluous.*

Guy Vialis appears to have been the first to have had the idea of producing luxury knives for wine-waiters. He thus invented Château Laguiole, a handsome bottle-opening knife whose coverings can be made of boxwood, bone, or carbon (see facing page). Other makes produced some excellent examples, such as those opposite from the Forges de Laguiole.

From East to West, people have always needed food and drink. As proof of these two necessities, here are two very different styles of pocket knife serving the same vital function.

Unless food is picked up on the knifepoint or in the fingers, eating a meal with a pocket knife is something of a challenge. Here, the principle of the eighteenth-century companion knife has been revived in the form of a picnic knife and fork. They are made by Hubertus, a well-known cutler from Solingen, Germany.

This model designed to aid the disabled eater probably dates from the end of the First World War. It consists of a fork and a knife on the same blade, so that it can be used by a person with only one hand.

This is the same idea as on the previous page—a complete table setting in a single implement. This high-quality Spanish version is made by Altor of Ermua in the province of Vizcaya.

The knife on the facing page is all of a piece, but here the set is divided in two. There is even a table-spoon, which can barely be seen in this illustration. The coverings may be made of plastic or wood.

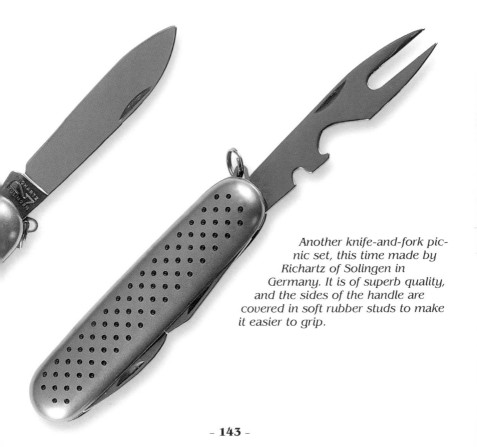

Another knife-and-fork picnic set, this time made by
Richartz of Solingen in
Germany. It is of superb quality,
and the sides of the handle are
covered in soft rubber studs to make
it easier to grip.

This set from the 1950s consists simply of one knife and one fork. The linings are of attractively marbled plastic.

This knife is one of the strokes of genius of the cutlery trade, a model specifically made for picking wild mushrooms. The Italians are the masters who produced this knife. It has a brush at the handle end for removing soil on the spot from your finds.

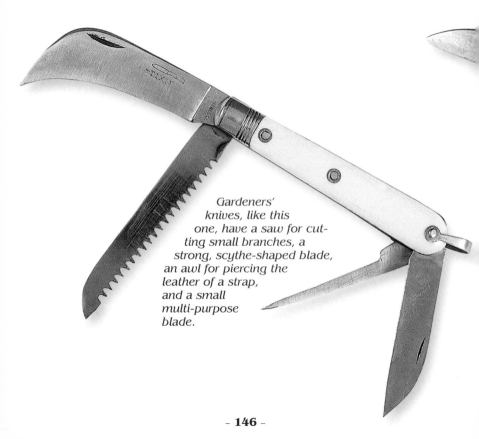

Gardeners' knives, like this one, have a saw for cutting small branches, a strong, scythe-shaped blade, an awl for piercing the leather of a strap, and a small multi-purpose blade.

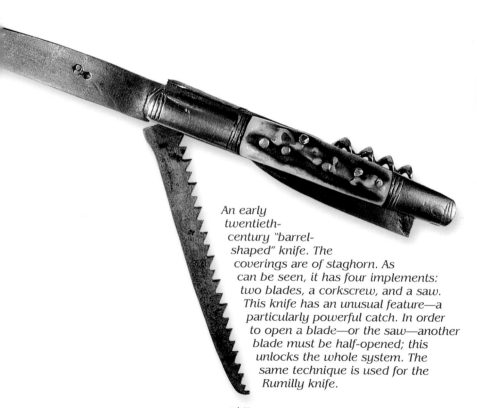

An early twentieth-century "barrel-shaped" knife. The coverings are of staghorn. As can be seen, it has four implements: two blades, a corkscrew, and a saw. This knife has an unusual feature—a particularly powerful catch. In order to open a blade—or the saw—another blade must be half-opened; this unlocks the whole system. The same technique is used for the Rumilly knife.

The Italians have been making wine for even longer than the French. Although the French also produce knives especially for use in vineyards, this one is Italian. The distinctive shape of the blade is ideal for pruning and thinning vines. The handle covering is blond horn.

This type of knife is known as Rouennais, from the town of Rouen in Normandy, a part of France famous for its sheep and cattle. The Rouennais was made in the region for centuries, but the local industry died out, and the knife is now made in Thiers. Note the strong blade and the other, thinner one fitted with a pennon for bleeding horses.

This folding scythe,
whose handle is of
cowhorn, is known as a
gouzette or gouzotte. It
originates from Burgundy, in
France. It is the utilitarian tool par
excellence, the faithful companion of
the grape-grower and the farmer. The
blade is made of recycled steel, no doubt
forged by a local blacksmith or farrier.

This is a handsome example of a basket-weaver's knife. The handle is of hard wood and has a splitter in the base. The blade is slightly curved and designed for cutting and stripping willow. Once the basket-maker has trimmed a piece of willow with the blade, he uses the splitter to divide it into three long strips.

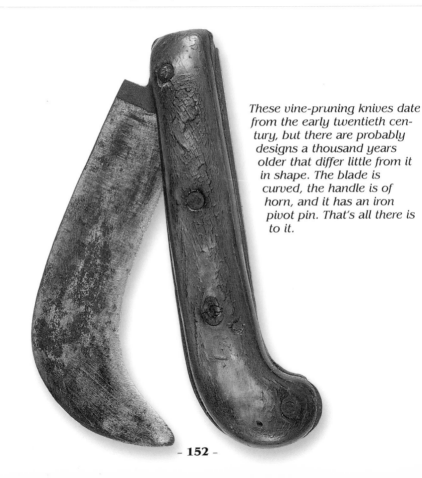

These vine-pruning knives date from the early twentieth century, but there are probably designs a thousand years older that differ little from it in shape. The blade is curved, the handle is of horn, and it has an iron pivot pin. That's all there is to it.

The horn on the vine-pruning knife on the facing page is used as a covering over iron linings, but this is a knife made of solid horn, with no bolsters.

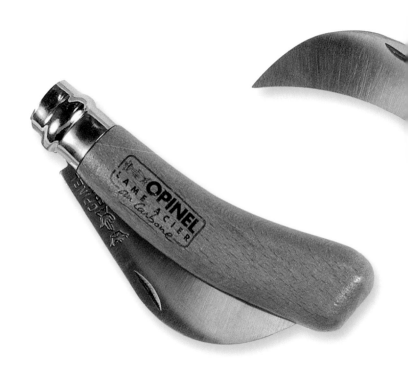

Opinel, a French firm that has produced thousands of Savoyard-type folding knives, extended its range a few years ago. It now makes folding gardener's pruning-knives in two shapes of blade, with different curvatures. There are also Opinel saw-bladed knives and folding saws that gardeners can keep in the pocket of their gardening apron.

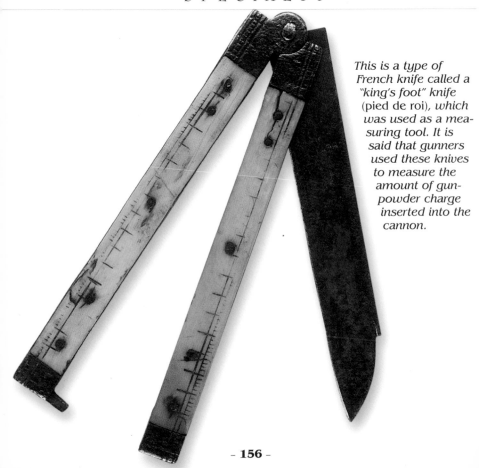

This is a type of French knife called a "king's foot" knife (pied de roi), which was used as a measuring tool. It is said that gunners used these knives to measure the amount of gunpowder charge inserted into the cannon.

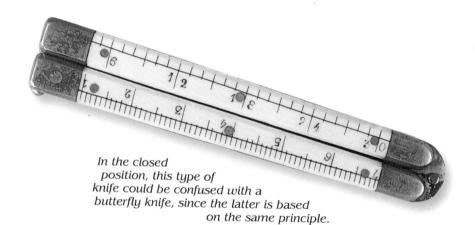

In the closed
position, this type of
knife could be confused with a
butterfly knife, since the latter is based
on the same principle.

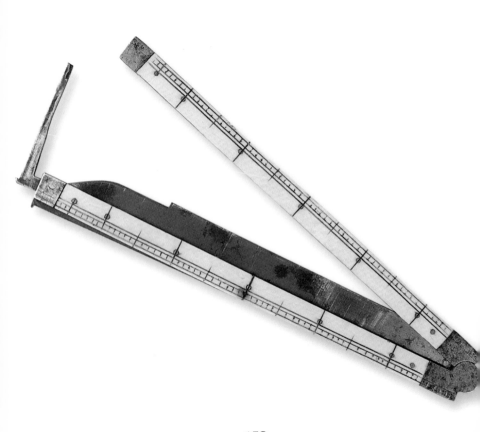

This is an eighteenth-century "king's foot" knife, combining a graduated ruler with an elegant steel blade. Like those on the preceding pages, these knives have ivory coverings and nickel silver bolsters. The foot in question is the same size as the foot that survives in American and imperial measurements (30.484 cm). However, the model on the right must be of a later date, as it uses the metric system of centimeters and millimeters.

Since everyone always needed a knife
with small blades suited for a multitude of
purposes—even if merely to keep a goose
quill pen sharp—these
good-looking pocket
knives were made with
any number of uses in
mind. But why so many
blades? So that one was
always sharp enough, of course!

This French knife has two blades and comes in a leather sheath. One blade is steel and the other solid silver. The coatings are of tortoiseshell and decorated with a shield. It dates from Napoleonic times.

Knives made for gentlemen in the eighteenth and early nineteenth centuries often had two blades made of two different materials, steel to cut meat and other foods, and solid silver for cutting fruits, since these were acidic. Steel reacts badly to acidic foods.

This knife is known as a "La Berge," for the French cutler who invented and patented it. This model is Italian and consists of a steel blade for cutting meats and solid foods and a fruit-knife blade in silver.

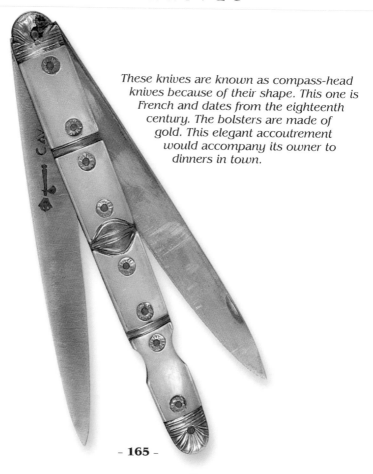

These knives are known as compass-head knives because of their shape. This one is French and dates from the eighteenth century. The bolsters are made of gold. This elegant accoutrement would accompany its owner to dinners in town.

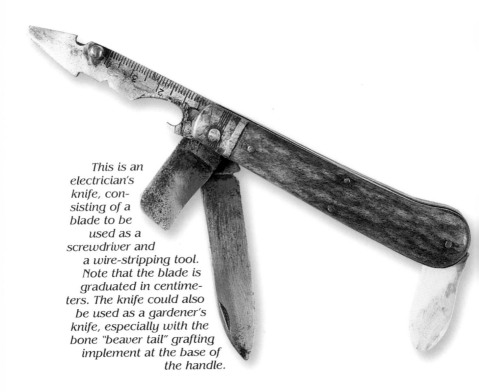

This is an electrician's knife, consisting of a blade to be used as a screwdriver and a wire-stripping tool. Note that the blade is graduated in centimeters. The knife could also be used as a gardener's knife, especially with the bone "beaver tail" grafting implement at the base of the handle.

Another gardener's knife, this time purpose-made, with a scythe-type pruning blade, a Yatagan blade, and beaver tail grafting implement at the tip. Note how the handle narrows in the center.

An attractive pair of knives with ivory coverings. The knives are multi-purpose, but they demonstrate the fact that a single knife blade is never enough.

These little knives are known as "mutton bones" on account of their shape. This one was probably made in Belgium and has ten attachments, including six blades of various sizes for cutting quills, opening letters, and performing all sorts of tasks. There is also a striking-iron or flint. The coverings are mother-of-pearl, and the knife dates from the early nineteenth century.

Every era has had its share of bizarre inventions. There were some great ones in the seventeenth century, such as these two pistol-shaped knives that do a lot more than just cut. They can also be used as bells, to strike a light, to seal a letter... The one thing they cannot do is shoot!

The steel in these knives is damascened in silver and gold. They are of German origin (Musée Le Secq des Tournelles, Rouen).

Jacques Mongin created this magnificent nautical knife that is only made in one size. It holds a strong blade, a marlinspike, and an unshackler.

Henri Viallon designed this knife for the firm of Pradel-Brossard, which has been producing inexpensive knives since time immemorial. The blade is stainless steel, and the large slot in it is used as an unshackler. The handle is made of a salt-resistant synthetic material, since it is for use at sea.

These are small schoolboy pocket knives, the sort that are blunt enough to do no real damage to little fingers. The coverings are in pastel colors to match the crayons, and their owners keep them in their pencil-cases, dreaming of longer blades—of the kind carried by swashbucklers…

Eka is a Swedish pocket-knife maker, based at Eskilstuna. It has been manufacturing since 1882 and has always put the emphasis on quality. This handsome model that dates from the 1950s has a corkscrew as well as three blades of different sizes and an unusual design of cigar-cutter. The tip of the cigar is inserted into the round hole in the handle, and the blade is folded back into the handle to cut the cigar. The covering is of engraved steel.

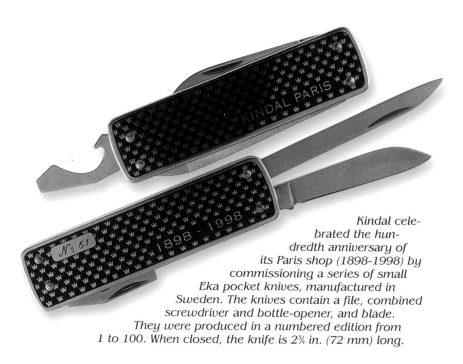

Kindal celebrated the hundredth anniversary of its Paris shop (1898-1998) by commissioning a series of small Eka pocket knives, manufactured in Sweden. The knives contain a file, combined screwdriver and bottle-opener, and blade. They were produced in a numbered edition from 1 to 100. When closed, the knife is 2¾ in. (72 mm) long.

This is another example of Swedish cutlery, this time from the 1920s. All the parts are made of steel. Note the button-hook.

*These
small, extra-flat
steel pocket knives are
manicure sets, containing all
the implements required for elegant
hands. They are Swedish, made by Eka, and are
still sold by Kindal, as they have been for decades, in their
handsome shop on the Avenue de l'Opéra in Paris. Note the
Celtic knot decoration on the bottom example.*

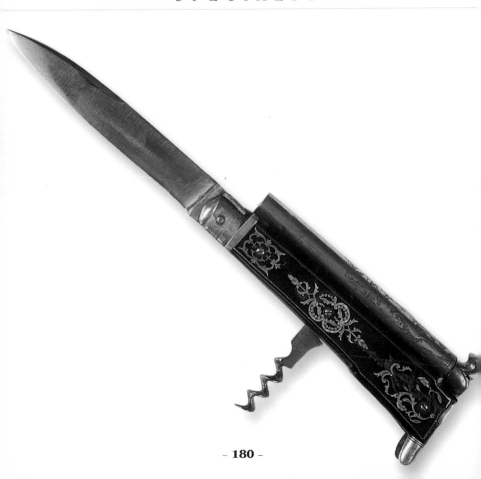

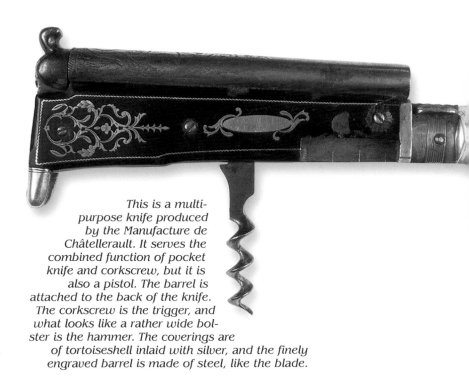

This is a multi-purpose knife produced by the Manufacture de Châtellerault. It serves the combined function of pocket knife and corkscrew, but it is also a pistol. The barrel is attached to the back of the knife. The corkscrew is the trigger, and what looks like a rather wide bolster is the hammer. The coverings are of tortoiseshell inlaid with silver, and the finely engraved barrel is made of steel, like the blade.

Many pocket knives, such as this one, conceal a hidden extra. In this case, it is difficult to decide whether this is a knife to which a revolver has been added, or a revolver fitted with a blade. It is an early twentieth-century model made in Thiers by Sigaud.

The Thiers
cutlery museum
contains many proto-
type models that were
designed to protect the
patent-holder from forgeries
and illegal copies of his work.
That is how this pair-of-scissors-
cum-pocket knife has survived, since
it appears not to have enjoyed much
commercial success.

The archetype of the multi-purpose Swiss knife is the Swiss Camp by Victorinox. It has twelve standard functions—large blade, small blade, corkscrew, can-opener, and so on, combining to perform a total of thirty-three functions. Note the plain hook at the bottom of the photo that looks like a button-hook for fastening boot buttons, but which has been adapted for more modern purposes such as holding a packet by the string.

These fob pocket knives, designed to be hung on a chain or fob, were fashionable between 1900 and the 1920s. Note the miniature scissors and tiny corkscrew to be used for removing corks from perfume flasks. These little pocket knives were mainly made in Nogent, France.

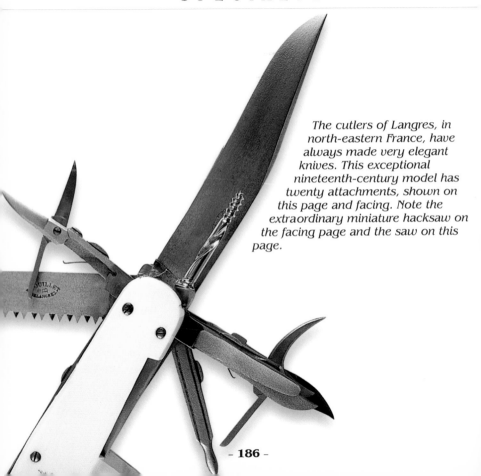

The cutlers of Langres, in north-eastern France, have always made very elegant knives. This exceptional nineteenth-century model has twenty attachments, shown on this page and facing. Note the extraordinary miniature hacksaw on the facing page and the saw on this page.

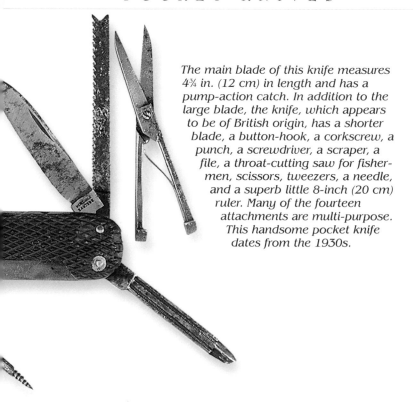

The main blade of this knife measures 4¾ in. (12 cm) in length and has a pump-action catch. In addition to the large blade, the knife, which appears to be of British origin, has a shorter blade, a button-hook, a corkscrew, a punch, a screwdriver, a scraper, a file, a throat-cutting saw for fishermen, scissors, tweezers, a needle, and a superb little 8-inch (20 cm) ruler. Many of the fourteen attachments are multi-purpose. This handsome pocket knife dates from the 1930s.

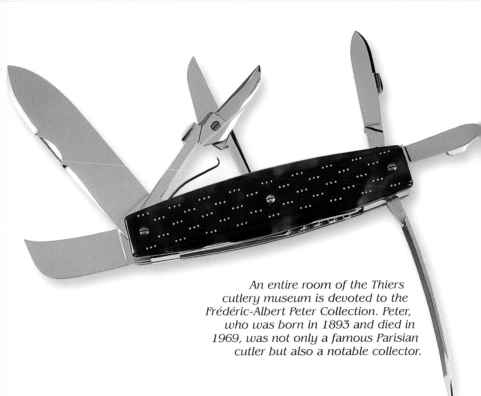

An entire room of the Thiers cutlery museum is devoted to the Frédéric-Albert Peter Collection. Peter, who was born in 1893 and died in 1969, was not only a famous Parisian cutler but also a notable collector.

*Peter's pocket
knives were made
of the finest materials
and were miniature works of
art in terms of quality and
precision. This model has
tortoiseshell coverings.*

*This handsome horseman's knife, which bears
Peter's mark, includes a hoof-trimmer, a
diestamp, a needle, and an awl
for repairing leather.*

The horseman's knife
on the facing page has
coverings of horn. This one,
also made by Peter, has
staghorn coverings. This knife is
more suitable for a gardener,
though clearly an upmarket one!

*Like the knife
on page 192, this
multi-functional knife is
destined especially for the
horseman, but in this case he is a
hunter. It is an elegant British knife
marked Butler and Co., dating from the
1950s, and including an unusual
attachment: a shotgun cartridge extractor.*

This typical product of Sheffield, England, has two blades, a hoof-trimmer and a corkscrew. The coverings are of mother-of-pearl.

This pocket knife of English manufacture could never have been intended to be kept in the pocket. It is so heavy and so large that no pocket lining would have withstood its weight for more than two days! This was probably a display piece made especially to grace the storefront window of a silverware showroom. It was made in the nineteenth century, and the coverings are of hand-engraved solid silver.

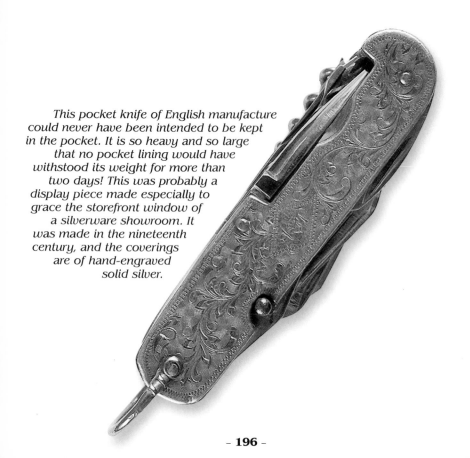

This is the same knife viewed from the side. Note the outsize fob ring, and count the number of attachments: seven on one side, eighteen in all! Proof, if any were needed, that the Swiss army knife is not a new invention.

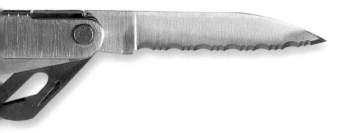

Many cutlery manufacturers have been com-
pletely carried away in their enthusiasm for
making tool attachments
for their knives.
Based on the example
of the Swiss army
knife, this ingenious
instrument contains a dozen
attachments, including two blades,
one of them with a serrated edge. The
American firm of Leatherman seems to have
been the first in this field, and produced tools
of excellent quality. Since then, Victorinox,
Gerber, Buck, and many others have followed
its example.

III

UNUSUAL
pocket knives

E very trade, every occupation, and every craft has its own style of pocket knife, designed for a specific purpose, for a well-defined task to be performed when the owner of the knife is away from home. But over time, cutlers wanted to do more, and tempt potential buyers with additional features. The idea was to amuse, surprise, and amaze the customer, who would be able to show off this clever invention to his friends. Thus jack-knives and switch-blades were invented, with new mechanisms, different from those of the clasp-knife.

*These could be called trick knives or clock knives.
There is a secret in knowing how to open and close
them. Some, such as this example dating from the
eighteenth century, have two clock faces on one side.
Others have yet another clock face on the other side of
the handle. The only way to open them is to set the
hands on the clock to a specified time.*

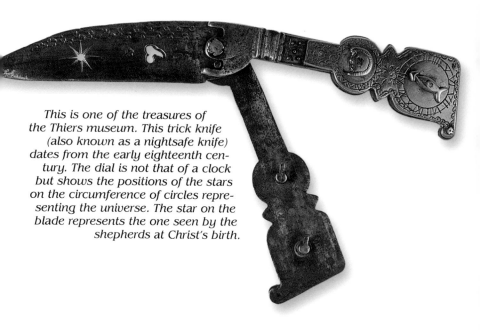

This is one of the treasures of
the Thiers museum. This trick knife
(also known as a nightsafe knife)
dates from the early eighteenth century. The dial is not that of a clock
but shows the positions of the stars
on the circumference of circles representing the universe. The star on the
blade represents the one seen by the
shepherds at Christ's birth.

*Trick knives were
all the rage among the
nobility and wealthy bourgeoisie
in eighteenth-century France. It should
not be forgotten that this was the era when
people were most eager for knowledge, and many
scientific and technical discoveries were made.*

During this period, each knife was a unique creation. This enlargement of the mechanisms shows the inscriptions engraved on brass.

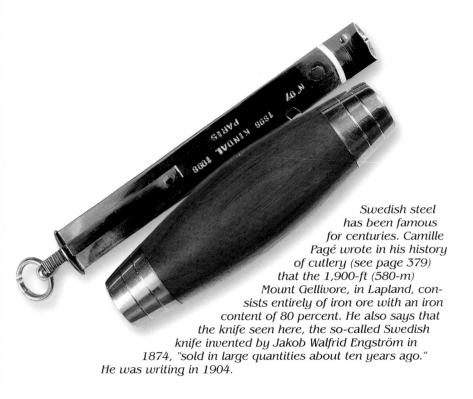

Swedish steel has been famous for centuries. Camille Pagé wrote in his history of cutlery (see page 379) that the 1,900-ft (580-m) Mount Gellivore, in Lapland, consists entirely of iron ore with an iron content of 80 percent. He also says that the knife seen here, the so-called Swedish knife invented by Jakob Walfrid Engström in 1874, "sold in large quantities about ten years ago." He was writing in 1904.

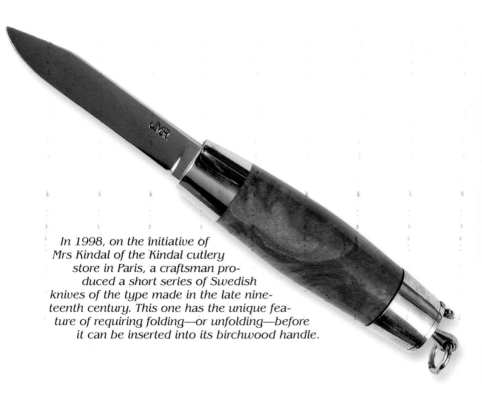

In 1998, on the initiative of
Mrs Kindal of the Kindal cutlery
store in Paris, a craftsman produced a short series of Swedish
knives of the type made in the late nineteenth century. This one has the unique feature of requiring folding—or unfolding—before
it can be inserted into its birchwood handle.

Jean-Michel Remaud, the craftsman who made the Swedish knife shown on the preceding page, created other excellent designs, including the barrel-shaped Secret model. The blade is hidden in the handle, and the slot is then concealed by a covering so that there is no hint of what lies inside.

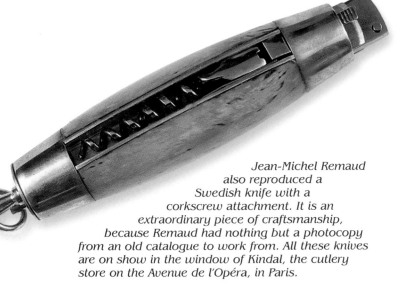

*Jean-Michel Remaud
also reproduced a
Swedish knife with a
corkscrew attachment. It is an
extraordinary piece of craftsmanship,
because Remaud had nothing but a photocopy
from an old catalogue to work from. All these knives
are on show in the window of Kindal, the cutlery
store on the Avenue de l'Opéra, in Paris.*

Another shape of folding knife, fashionable in northern India, opens in three stages. When closed, it is perfectly safe, even deep in a pocket.

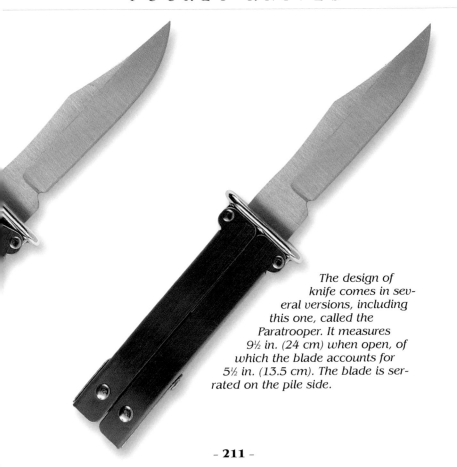

The design of knife comes in several versions, including this one, called the Paratrooper. It measures 9½ in. (24 cm) when open, of which the blade accounts for 5½ in. (13.5 cm). The blade is serrated on the pile side.

This French folding knife was made by Jean-Pierre Treille in the late 1980s. As can be seen, the blade pivots and folds back flat into the handle. There is a catch, visible in the photograph, that holds the blade firmly in the open or closed position.

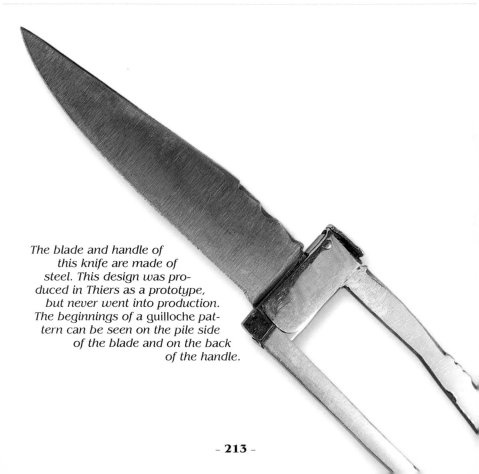

The blade and handle of this knife are made of steel. This design was produced in Thiers as a prototype, but never went into production. The beginnings of a guilloche pattern can be seen on the pile side of the blade and on the back of the handle.

This American model is similar in design to the knife on the preceding page, but this time the safety-catch has been replaced by a stud that holds the blade in place when fully open or closed.

This stainless steel knife, made by Mountain Forge of Cleveland, Georgia, has the great advantage of being extra-flat.

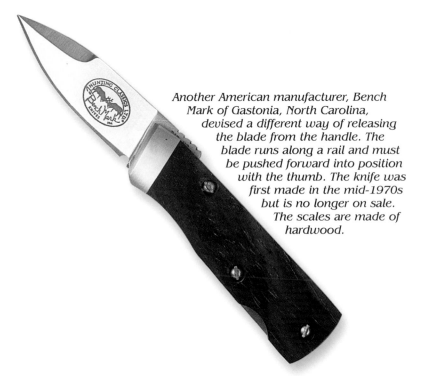

Another American manufacturer, Bench Mark of Gastonia, North Carolina, devised a different way of releasing the blade from the handle. The blade runs along a rail and must be pushed forward into position with the thumb. The knife was first made in the mid-1970s but is no longer on sale. The scales are made of hardwood.

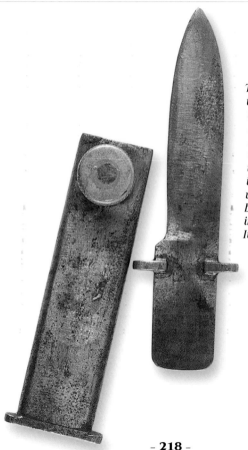

This is a prototype of a knife that closes but is not a folding knife, because the blade must be detached from the handle before it can be inserted into it. A large thumbwheel holds the blade in place when the knife is in use, and also secures the blade when it is put back into its sheath-cum-handle. It was designed by Jean-Pierre Treille around 1970

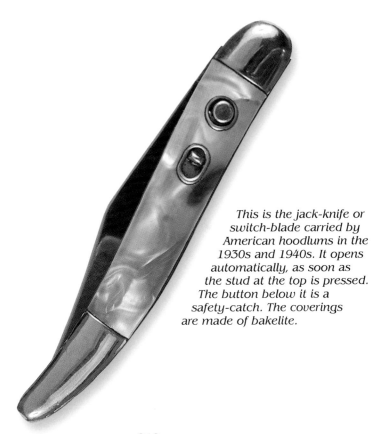

This is the jack-knife or switch-blade carried by American hoodlums in the 1930s and 1940s. It opens automatically, as soon as the stud at the top is pressed. The button below it is a safety-catch. The coverings are made of bakelite.

Jack-knives and flick-knives were first made in the nineteenth century. This is a handsome example from the French town of Châtellerault. The coverings are of mother-of-pearl, the bolsters and guard are of nickel silver. There is a safety-catch just below the push-button mechanism.

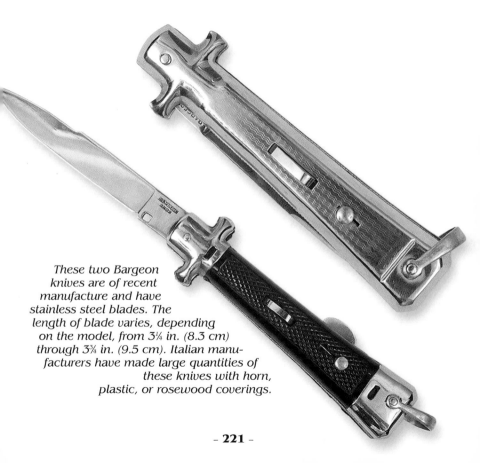

These two Bargeon knives are of recent manufacture and have stainless steel blades. The length of blade varies, depending on the model, from 3¼ in. (8.3 cm) through 3¾ in. (9.5 cm). Italian manufacturers have made large quantities of these knives with horn, plastic, or rosewood coverings.

This is another automatic knife, but on this one, the blade is pushed straight out along the line of the handle. Called Le Superoto, it is made by Douris & Chastel. The stainless steel blade measures 3 ¾ in. (9.5 cm) long and is exposed when the black slide is pushed along its slot on the handle.

This is a similar design by the American firm of Cold Steel, but manufactured in Japan. It has a safety-catch.

The firm of Douris & Chastel at Thiers in France make switch-blades such as this one.

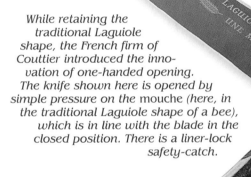

While retaining the traditional Laguiole shape, the French firm of Couttier introduced the innovation of one-handed opening. The knife shown here is opened by simple pressure on the mouche (here, in the traditional Laguiole shape of a bee), which is in line with the blade in the closed position. There is a liner-lock safety-catch.

IV

MODERN

pocket knives

Over the centuries, pocket knives have undergone an almost Darwinian process of evolution and selection. Modern knives, such as those shown on the following pages, often look dangerous, but are usually well-provided with safety-catches. Today, there are many specialist dealers and collector's clubs all over Europe and North America who are happy to provide advice and support to the novice pocket knife collector. And fortunately, there are still a few enthusiasts and artisan-cutlers who continue to make superb, hand-crafted examples in the true tradition of the Age of Enlightenment.

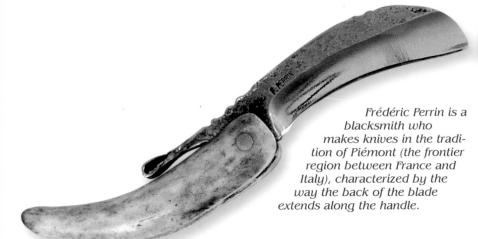

Frédéric Perrin is a blacksmith who makes knives in the tradition of Piémont (the frontier region between France and Italy), characterized by the way the back of the blade extends along the handle.

Pascal Graveline
is a true artist. His
specialty is making
rare and superb reproduc-
tions of classic knives. He
even makes his own blades, in
stainless steel, using the metal
removal method. The knife on the
far right is known as a friend's
knife because it can be split in
two, to be lent to a friend, during
a meal for instance. The knife on
the near right is known as a violin
knife, on account of its shape.

Laurent Gaillard, a
craftsman from the Landes region of
France, is a fine blacksmith, so the
trademark he uses to sign his blades is
an anvil. The handles are made of various types of wood, such as yew,
boxwood, or walnut.

Ludovic Marsille is proud of his Breton heritage and makes his knives in the traditional local style. The handle of his Kontellig is made of turned wood.

This is another version of the Sauveterre type made by Vialis, shown on page 80. This one has an ivory handle and a damascened blade made by Dourcin.

This knife is made by Bignon. The blade is of D2 stainless steel, and the handle is made of bog-oak, a rare type of fossilized wood found only in swamps.

This handsome model made by Veysseyre, one of the best cutlers in Thiers, is called Cranios. The bolsters and blade are damascened and the coverings are of polished staghorn.

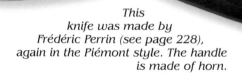

*This
knife was made by
Frédéric Perrin (see page 228),
again in the Piémont style. The handle
is made of horn.*

A South African
craftsman produced
this knife whose blade is
of WL4116 stainless steel. The
coverings are of tropical wood inlaid with
a pattern of arabesques. The knife is operated by
a pump-action mechanism.

Veysseyre called this model Fred, as a tribute to his good friend and fellow cutler, Frédéric Perrin. The handle is covered in warthog tusk, the blade is damascened in a leaf pattern, and the bolster is mosaic pattern Damascus work. Even the fob attachment is damascened. An amazing piece of craftsmanship!

The French firm of
Couttier created this knife
that can be opened with one
hand, by pressing on the small
stud on the tang of the blade. The
catch is also interesting in its simplici-
ty. A very thin leaf-spring, that can just
be seen running down the top part of the
handle, holds the blade in place when it is
open. When this is pushed with the thumb
the blade is released, and it will then drop
under the influence of gravity.

Bignon
offers this
model called
Marius. Its blade
is machined from
a strip of D2 stainless
steel, by grinding away
the metal. The handle coverings are of olive wood.

Another one-handed switch-blade made by the French firm of Florinox. The button used for opening it is on the back of the handle. The coverings are inlaid with mother-of-pearl in the Asiatic style.

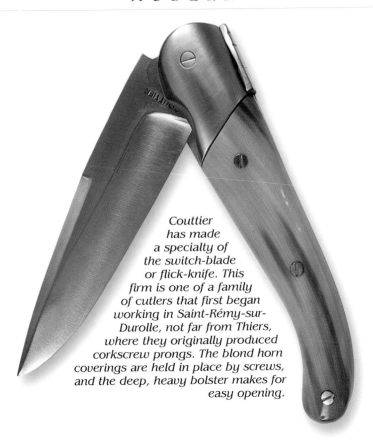

*Couttier
has made
a specialty of
the switch-blade
or flick-knife. This
firm is one of a family
of cutlers that first began
working in Saint-Rémy-sur-
Durolle, not far from Thiers,
where they originally produced
corkscrew prongs. The blond horn
coverings are held in place by screws,
and the deep, heavy bolster makes for
easy opening.*

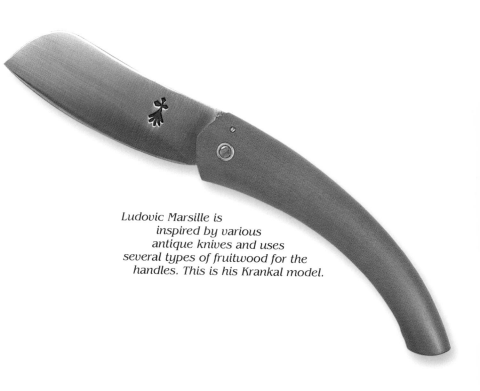

Ludovic Marsille is inspired by various antique knives and uses several types of fruitwood for the handles. This is his Krankal model.

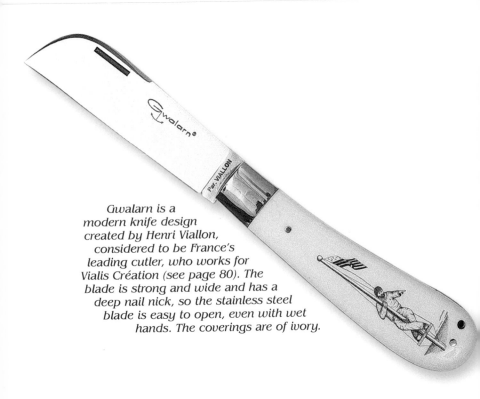

Gwalarn is a
modern knife design
created by Henri Viallon,
considered to be France's
leading cutler, who works for
Vialis Création (see page 80). The
blade is strong and wide and has a
deep nail nick, so the stainless steel
blade is easy to open, even with wet
hands. The coverings are of ivory.

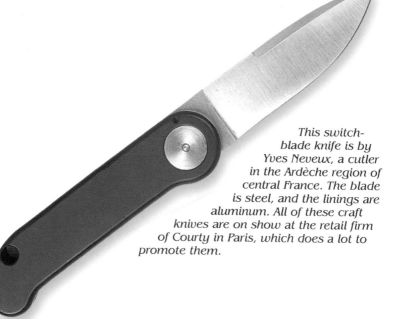

This switch-blade knife is by Yves Neveux, a cutler in the Ardèche region of central France. The blade is steel, and the linings are aluminum. All of these craft knives are on show at the retail firm of Courty in Paris, which does a lot to promote them.

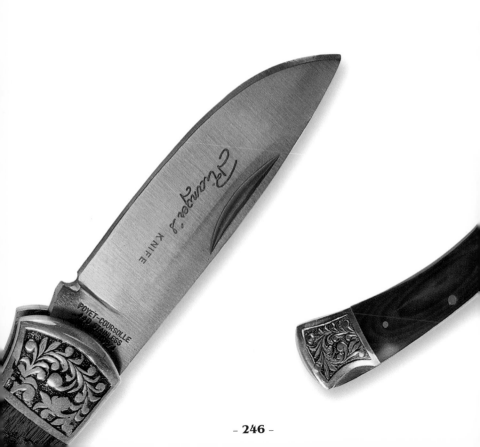

Rangers is a trademark of the French firm of Coursolle. The knives are inspired by Buck knives but are in a lower price range.

The blades of these
German-made Herbertz pump-
action knives are of 440 stainless
steel. They are 4 in. (10 cm) long. The
handles may have one or two bolsters,
and there is a choice of two styles
of engraving.

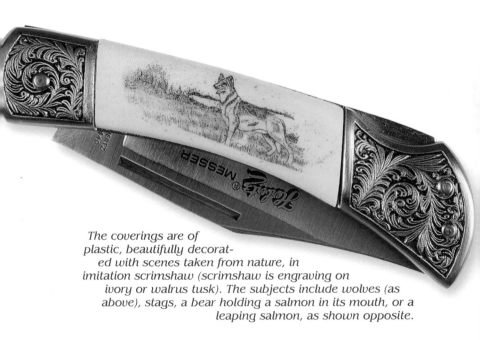

The coverings are of plastic, beautifully decorated with scenes taken from nature, in imitation scrimshaw (scrimshaw is engraving on ivory or walrus tusk). The subjects include wolves (as above), stags, a bear holding a salmon in its mouth, or a leaping salmon, as shown opposite.

Arplex offers a
range of jack-knives
made in Asia. The designs
are inspired by traditional
American favorites such as Buck. The
blades are made of 420 stainless steel
with a low carbon content. This means they
are particularly adapted to maritime use, as
this grade of steel is less subject to corrosion
than high-carbon steels.

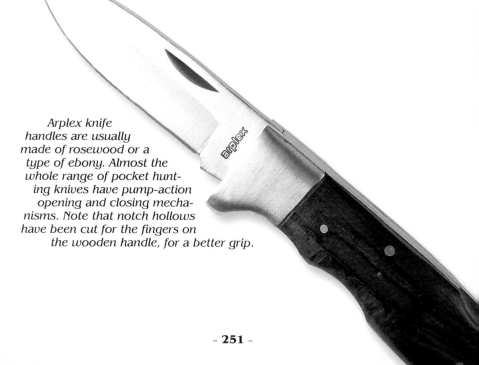

Arplex knife handles are usually made of rosewood or a type of ebony. Almost the whole range of pocket hunting knives have pump-action opening and closing mechanisms. Note that notch hollows have been cut for the fingers on the wooden handle, for a better grip.

This handsome pocket knife is American-made. It is extra-flat and so very suitable for carrying around.

William Henry is a U.S. manufacturer of custom knives. These are two of the best examples of his work. The coverings are of planed staghorn.

The Maison des Couteliers in Thiers produces very elegant knives in short production runs. This is Profil, a pocket knife with a wrist-strap. The ironwood coverings have a lovely sheen. The blade is stainless steel.

This frame-lock knife, produced by the Columbia River Knife and Tool Company, is called K.I.S.S. The blade, handle, and clip are all made of steel.

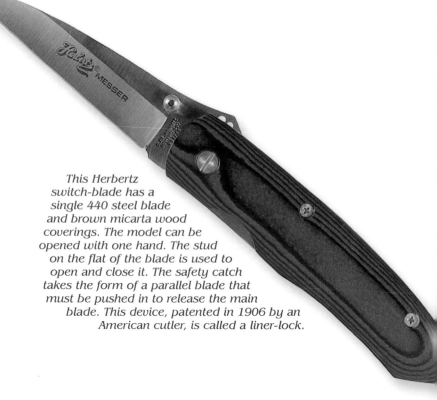

This Herbertz
switch-blade has a
single 440 steel blade
and brown micarta wood
coverings. The model can be
opened with one hand. The stud
on the flat of the blade is used to
open and close it. The safety catch
takes the form of a parallel blade that
must be pushed in to release the main
blade. This device, patented in 1906 by an
American cutler, is called a liner-lock.

The very com-
pact shape of this
knife is of Japanese
design. This Ranger
knife is a copy of the
Stubby but this one has pale
horn coverings, unlike
the latter, whose handle is made
entirely of aluminum.

*Böker
makes
many different
models of these
pump-action knives
that are traditionally
used as hunting knives.*

This is the
Echo model
made by the
Columbia River Knife and
Tool Company (CRKT). It
comes complete with a nylon
sheath for attaching to a belt. The
blade is in the Japanese tanto shape.
The handle is made of plastic.

This is another
one-handed knife,
manufactured by
Gigand, but designed by
the American, Fred Carter. It
is an extra-flat knife. The blade
has several catches on which to
position the thumb.

This is one of the
Spyderco range, fea-
turing several knives
with belt-clips or ring-
clips. The model shown here
is called Snap-it. The handle is
made of Zytel/kraton, a futuristic
name for a type of plastic. It measures
4 in. (10 cm), and the clasp is part of the
design. The blade is serrated.

It is easy to see why this knife has
been called a Spider, since both the pierced
blade and the handle are designed on the
theme of the spider and web. The blade may be
serrated or smooth. The knife is 3½ in. (8.5 cm) long.

Manufacturers of modern pocket knives tend to offer their customers a choice of smooth or serrated blades. The liner-lock is also coming into widespread use.

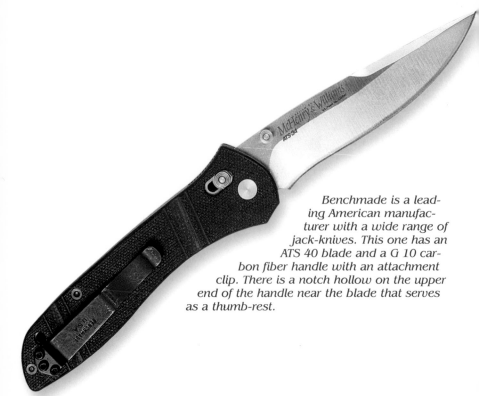

Benchmade is a leading American manufacturer with a wide range of jack-knives. This one has an ATS 40 blade and a G 10 carbon fiber handle with an attachment clip. There is a notch hollow on the upper end of the handle near the blade that serves as a thumb-rest.

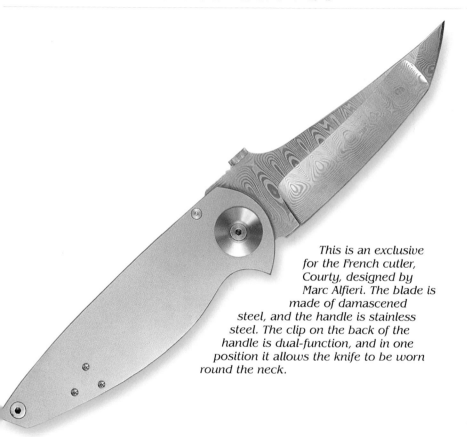

This is an exclusive for the French cutler, Courty, designed by Marc Alfieri. The blade is made of damascened steel, and the handle is stainless steel. The clip on the back of the handle is dual-function, and in one position it allows the knife to be worn round the neck.

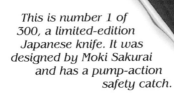

This is number 1 of
300, a limited-edition
Japanese knife. It was
designed by Moki Sakurai
and has a pump-action
safety catch.

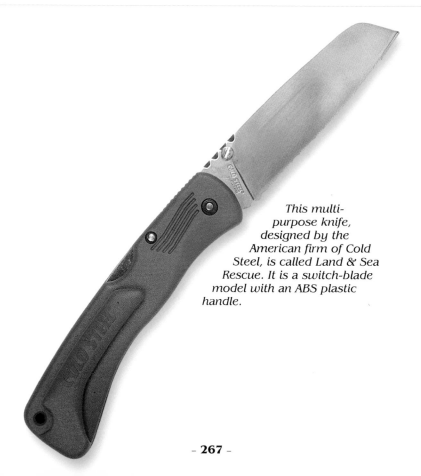

This multi-purpose knife, designed by the American firm of Cold Steel, is called Land & Sea Rescue. It is a switch-blade model with an ABS plastic handle.

This is a knife designed by Allen Elishewitz for Benchmade. It has a liner-lock, an operating button on the tang of the blade, and a pocket-clip—the archetypal modern-style knife.

This folding knife created by Marc Alfieri has a uniquely shaped, damascened, stainless steel blade and a handle covered in palmwood.

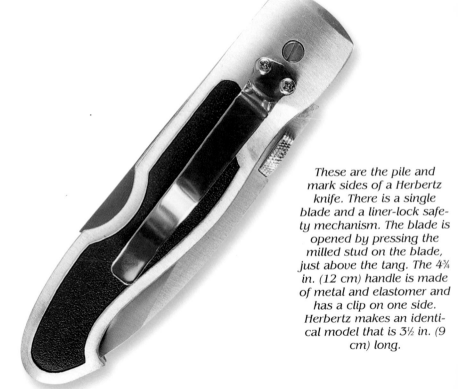

These are the pile and mark sides of a Herbertz knife. There is a single blade and a liner-lock safety mechanism. The blade is opened by pressing the milled stud on the blade, just above the tang. The 4¾ in. (12 cm) handle is made of metal and elastomer and has a clip on one side. Herbertz makes an identical model that is 3½ in. (9 cm) long.

*Another
German firm,
Böker, makes
numerous ver-
sions of these
Speedlock and Toplock knives.
They may be automatic or manual, and the steel blades may be
interchangeable. The blades may even be made of ceramic.*

Spyderco's great invention is this hole which is much easier to use than a nail nick for opening the blade. The blade is rotated effortlessly and safely between two fingers. The handle on this model is made of carbon fiber.

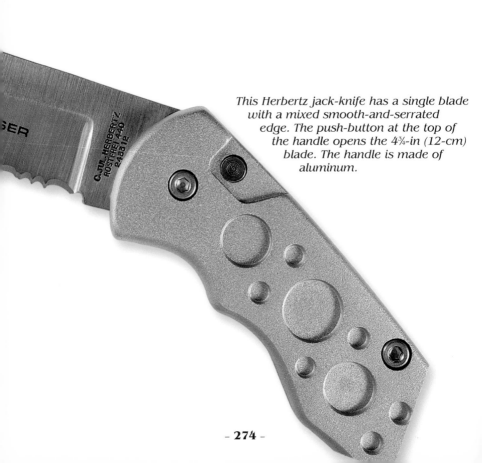

This Herbertz jack-knife has a single blade with a mixed smooth-and-serrated edge. The push-button at the top of the handle opens the 4¾-in (12-cm) blade. The handle is made of aluminum.

This Spyderco model
has a 5¼ in. (13 cm) blade
with a choice of smooth or
serrated edge.

This is no knife for such harmless pastimes as wild mushroom picking; the blade is designed for combat. This Cold Steel model exists in three sizes of which the largest is 13 in. (33 cm) long when the knife is open.

This collector's knife, produced in the 1990s, is signed by the Canadian artist José de Bragas. It has a safety catch, and the bolster is pulled out to release the blade. The angular bolster is made of titanium, and the attractive iridescent scales are of abalone shell.

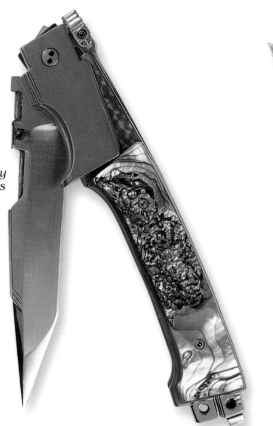

This handsome 3½ in. (9 cm) blade is marked Henri Viallon, a French maker. The handle coverings are made of mammoth ivory and held in place with screws. The bolster is in mosaic pattern Damascus work, and the blade has been damascened in a leaf-pattern.

This extraordinary creation by Larry Fuegen injects some humor into what is otherwise an all-too-serious art. Seen in profile, this is a classic, well-made knife with a damascened blade and staghorn handle. But the handle end has been carved to look like a monster with a movable tongue, shining eyes, and vampire teeth!

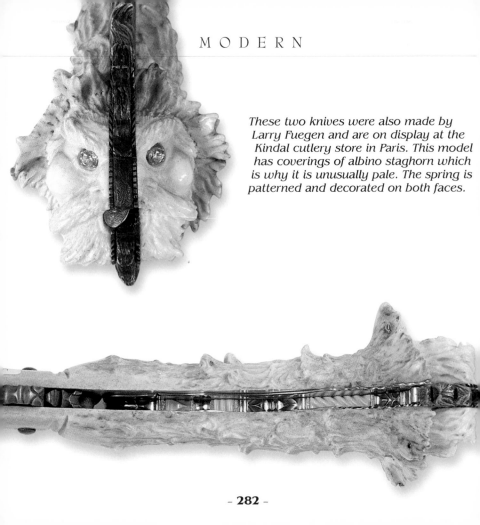

These two knives were also made by Larry Fuegen and are on display at the Kindal cutlery store in Paris. This model has coverings of albino staghorn which is why it is unusually pale. The spring is patterned and decorated on both faces.

Some cutlers have a style that sets them apart from the rest. This applies to Jean-Marc Laroche, who creates pocket knives inspired by strip cartoons of the 1970s and 1980s. They combine eroticism and elements of horror. This sculptured knife is called Erectus. It is made of resin with a nickel-plated steel blade.

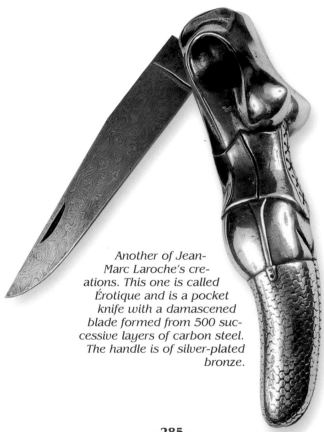

Another of Jean-Marc Laroche's creations. This one is called Érotique and is a pocket knife with a damascened blade formed from 500 successive layers of carbon steel. The handle is of silver-plated bronze.

V

FIGURATIVE
pocket knives

Over the years, people came to appreciate knives that were decorative as well as functional. That, at least, seems to be the message conveyed by specialty knives and those with figurative designs. Cutlers needed to add something special in order to be able to continue selling their wares. They could then sell a few—if not a lot—more.

This constant quest for new customers generated novelty pocket knives. Knives have long come in all sorts of unexpected shapes and sizes, including women's legs, bottles, fish, dogs, cats, and goodness knows what else!

A seventeenth-century, single-bladed knife with a thick blade back, held in place by a single pin. The carved ivory handle represents a nun. This most unusual knife, and the equally rare knife on the facing page, are on show at the cutlery museum in Thiers.

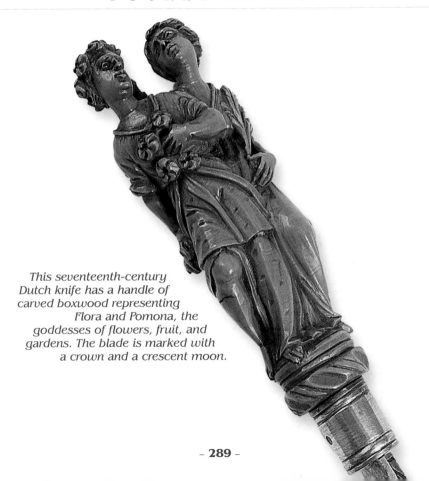

This seventeenth-century
Dutch knife has a handle of
carved boxwood representing
Flora and Pomona, the
goddesses of flowers, fruit, and
gardens. The blade is marked with
a crown and a crescent moon.

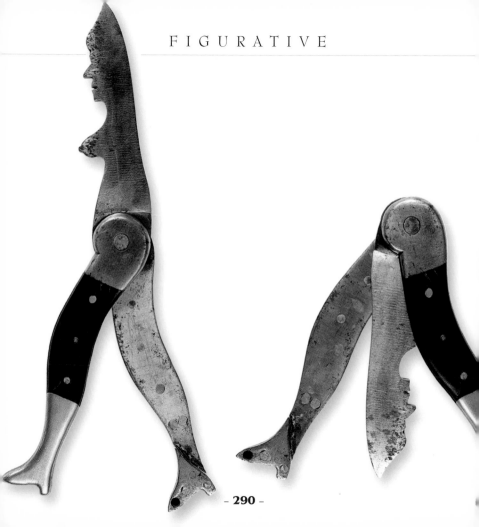

This extraordinary, anthropomorphic knife was made in the second half of the nineteenth century. Each of the three components pivots on an axis. A catch holds the knife open. To close it, the left leg has to be turned in a 360° circle, enabling the blade to return to the socket. The pocket knife is made of steel, brass, and horn.

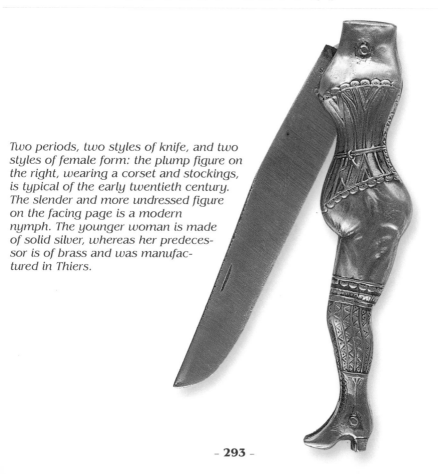

Two periods, two styles of knife, and two styles of female form: the plump figure on the right, wearing a corset and stockings, is typical of the early twentieth century. The slender and more undressed figure on the facing page is a modern nymph. The younger woman is made of solid silver, whereas her predecessor is of brass and was manufactured in Thiers.

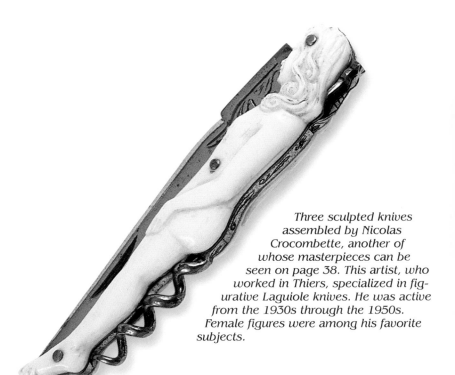

Three sculpted knives assembled by Nicolas Crocombette, another of whose masterpieces can be seen on page 38. This artist, who worked in Thiers, specialized in figurative Laguiole knives. He was active from the 1930s through the 1950s. Female figures were among his favorite subjects.

Two centuries of knife manufacture separate the modern
leg by Charles Couttier (above)
from the leg-shaped trick knife opposite. The small Couttier knife has boxwood coverings, those of the eighteenth-
century knife are of ivory. The linings and blade are
made of steel, the top bolster is of copper, and the
bottom bolster is of brass.

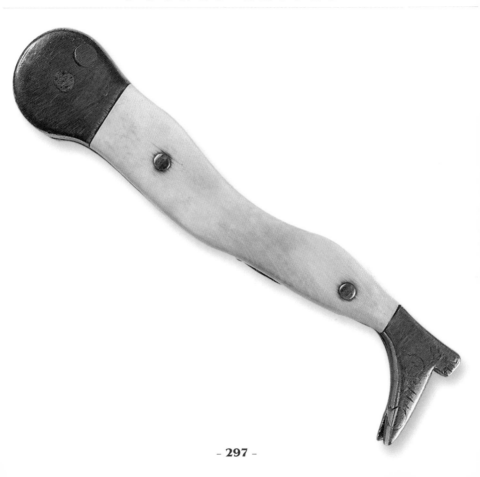

Women's shoes were as much of an inspiration as their legs. These two pocket knives were made in Thiers. One is of ivory, the other of pressed horn. This pocket knife was made for the firm of Bourgade-Tarry in the early twentieth century.

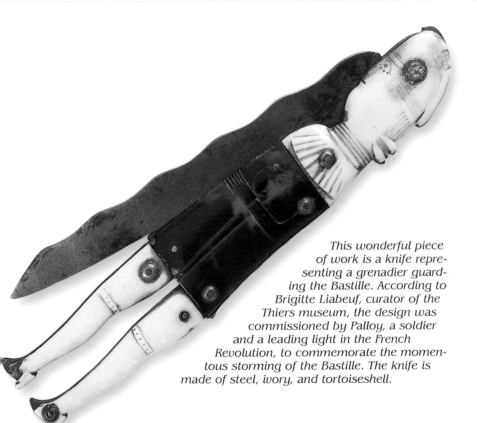

This wonderful piece of work is a knife representing a grenadier guarding the Bastille. According to Brigitte Liabeuf, curator of the Thiers museum, the design was commissioned by Palloy, a soldier and a leading light in the French Revolution, to commemorate the momentous storming of the Bastille. The knife is made of steel, ivory, and tortoiseshell.

If women's legs and feet have inspired cutlers, why not the legs and hooves of horses?

One of the registered prototypes (see page 183) is this writer's knife, whose handle contains a tiny pen and pencil.

This amusing skittle-shaped knife with three blades is another registered prototype (see page 183).

*This is another of the proto-
type models for registration. It is a calendar knife,
dating from 1861. All of these registered prototypes can
be seen in the Thiers cutlery museum.*

The strange knife on the left has two blades, and is shaped like a telescope. It dates from the early twentieth century. The two knives on the right, whose handles are shaped like grandfather clocks, belong in the figurative category. On one of them, the clock face has been replaced by a compass.

These early twentieth-century knives have handles of painted bone inspired by insects, a ladybug on the left and a moth on the right. Their blades are made of steel.

Like the small pocket knives on the previous two pages, the handle on this model is modeled on that of an insect, possibly a grasshopper. The handle is of ivory, and the blade is marked with the name of a retailer of Coulommiers knives.

This typically Italian knife, whose handle is engraved with a cherub and grapevines, is marked Ricordo, meaning "souvenir." It was made in Italy in the late nineteenth century. The small, slightly incurved blade is for cutting quill pens.

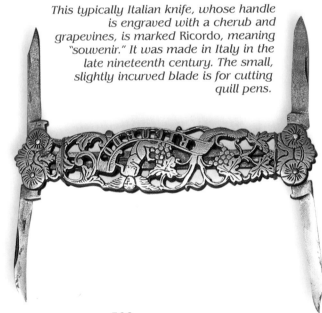

A blade—or two—
can be inserted
into almost any
shape, making the result
into a charming souvenir. Here are
three examples: a football, a lighthouse
and an ignition key, a 1950s promotional
item for the firm of Neiman.

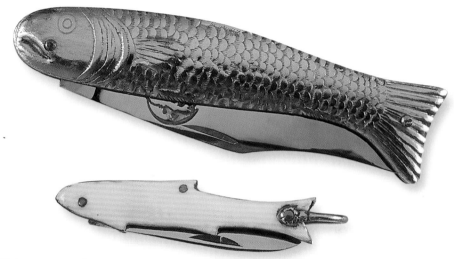

Fish are a popular
theme for pocket knives. After all,
their shape lends itself particularly well to the purpose.
The top one is by Batisse and has coverings of hammered
sheet-iron. The blade is marked with the maker's crescent
moon mark. The bottom knife has ivorine coverings.

Dogs, man's companion since time immemorial, are another popular subject for knife handles. These two models are on display in the Le Secq des Tournelles museum in Rouen, Normandy, and have horn and ivory coverings. The blades are made of steel. They date from the eighteenth century.

*This little
knife in the shape of a
running dog is of Spanish origin. It was made in
Saragossa, once the capital of the kingdom of
Aragon, hence the mark Zaragoza on the blade.
The end of the dog's tail has been broken off, but it
once formed a perfect circle by which the knife
could be attached to a fob or chain.*

This little pocket knife, dating from the early twentieth century, whose handle represents a sleeping dog, is more of a manicure set. It includes a nail file and a couple of steel blades. The coverings are of bakelite. The knife was made in Thiers, France.

This large Laguiole knife has fly-ing ducks beautifully carved on the boxwood linings of the handle. When open, it measures just over 12½ in. (32 cm).

This modern
Laguiole knife is made
by Le Berger. The bolsters at
the top on each side represent the left
and right profiles of a hunting dog,
which appears to be chasing the
ducks on the knife opposite!

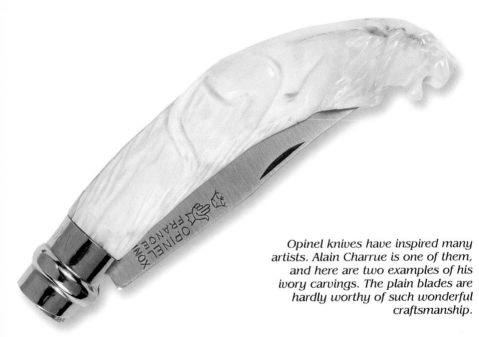

Opinel knives have inspired many artists. Alain Charrue is one of them, and here are two examples of his ivory carvings. The plain blades are hardly worthy of such wonderful craftsmanship.

It's amazing what
  you can find in the
    markets of China. In amongst various items of
kitchen equipment, you might discover these tiny pocket knives,
  most of which have pump-action mechanisms. Although the
  blades are of rather poor quality stainless steel, the handles are
  made of bronze. From left to right, there is a cow, a crocodile, a
  corn cob, a rat swallowing coins, and a peanut. These pocket
            knives are often attached to key-rings.

This superb piece of work is in the style of the Nogent and Éloi Pernet knives. A Louis XIV coin has been converted into a pocket manicure set. The coin may well date from the reign of the Sun King (eighteenth century), but the transformation dates only from the 1960s when this type of gadget was very much in vogue.

A great exhibition, known as the Exposition Universelle, was held in Paris in 1900. Two exhibition buildings that still stand, known as the Grand Palais and the Petit Palais, as well as the Alexander III bridge, were built for the occasion. One of the most popular souvenirs of the exhibition was a little pocket knife in the shape a nail. This is a play on words since the French word for "nail" (clou) means "highlight" or "success story." The coverings are made of aluminum, the blade is of steel, and the knife was made in Thiers.

Every famous city produces its share of souvenirs for sale to the tourists. One might assume that this gondola-shaped pocket knife, sold on its own or on a key-ring, came from Venice. Yet it might just as easily have been made in Thiers, France, as in Scarperia, Italy.

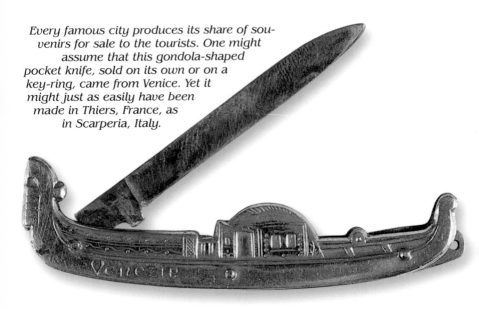

If you look closely, you will see a little hole on the first floor of the Eiffel Tower handle of this early twentieth-century pocket knife. If you looked through the hole and held the knife up to the light, you would be able to see a tiny photo of another of the sights of Paris.

The Eiffel Tower, designed by Gustave Eiffel, was built for the 1889 World Exhibition in Paris. Here are two more souvenir pocket knives dating from that time. On the left-hand knife, the little hole containing the tiny photograph (see the preceding page) is on the top floor of the tower. Both knives were made in Thiers and are decorated with heat-stamped horn.

This little knife is a piece of French propaganda from the latter half of the nineteenth century, the time of the Franco-Prussian War. One side of the handle represents a Prussian soldier, whose pointed helmet is extended by the open blade. The covering shows him wearing an enormous boot. The other side (not seen in this photograph) is a laughing French soldier. The knife was almost certainly made in Thiers.

This French cannon-shaped pocket knife probably dates from Napoleonic times. The linings are of bronze, and the single blade is of steel, as is the spring.

A talented cutler called Jean Verdier made this large hunting knife in the shape of a shotgun barrel around 1930. The blade is steel, and the coverings are of ivory and mahogany. Note on the bottom left-hand side of the handle there is a device for extracting the pin from cartridges.

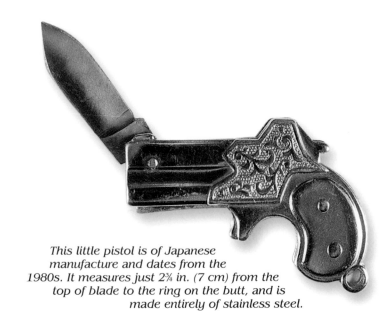

*This little pistol is of Japanese
manufacture and dates from the
1980s. It measures just 2¾ in. (7 cm) from the
top of blade to the ring on the butt, and is
made entirely of stainless steel.*

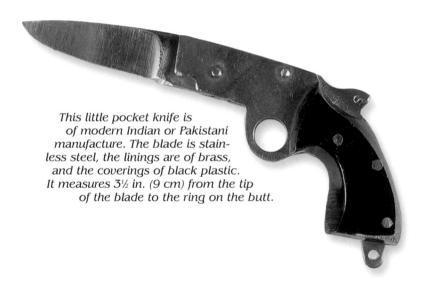

This little pocket knife is
of modern Indian or Pakistani
manufacture. The blade is stainless steel, the linings are of brass,
and the coverings of black plastic.
It measures 3½ in. (9 cm) from the tip
of the blade to the ring on the butt.

The black bakelite handle makes this look like a genuine automatic. In fact, it is indeed an automatic, but a switch-blade, not a pistol. The blade flicks out when the "trigger" is pulled. It is a French knife, made in Thiers in the 1950s.

This is a much more deadly weapon, a six-shooter made in Thiers in the late nineteenth century. The handle coverings are of horn, and the steel blade is the same shape as those found on Laguiole knives. Note the engraved decoration on the breechblock and the top of the barrel.

This registered model called Le Touriste has attachments that might come in handy for the traveler, including one large and one small blade, as well as a serious-looking corkscrew. It was made in Thiers, France, in the 1920s. The coverings are of ivory, and the figurative bolsters are of bronze.

This unusual three-bladed knife dates from the mid-nineteenth century. The figure depicted on the handle is that of Marshal Ney, Napoleon's general. The blades are of steel, and the coverings bronze.

Pocket knives are often made to commemorate an event or special occasion. This book contains a Laguiole knife made for the year 2000 (see page 54) and a pocket knife sold as a souvenir at the Paris Universal Exhibition of 1900 (see page 323). This particular knife was sold to commemorate the first non-stop, solo transatlantic flight by Charles Lindbergh in 1927. The blade is of steel, the coverings of stamped brass.

The word "souvenir" is clearly engraved on the handle of this knife that was probably made in Austria. The Austrians once had a flourishing cutlery industry, located in Styria, and their products were distributed all over the world, as is the case today with knives made in Thiers, France, and Solingen, Germany. The coverings are of aluminum, and the other side shows the back view of the mountaineer.

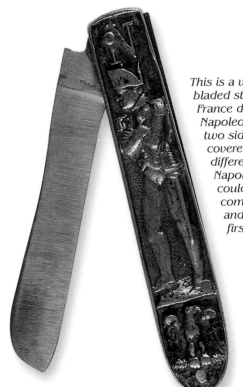

This is a very rare single-bladed steel knife made in France during the Napoleonic period. The two sides of the bronze-covered handle show different scenes and Napoleonic symbols. It could be classified as a commemorative knife and may even be the first of its kind.

Coursolle is
a very old cutlery firm in
Thiers, whose maker's mark
was a wrench. Proud of its
French manufacturing tradition, the company produced
a large series of these decorated knives which
represented various occu-
pations, such as farmers
and sportsmen. This one
features a boxer.

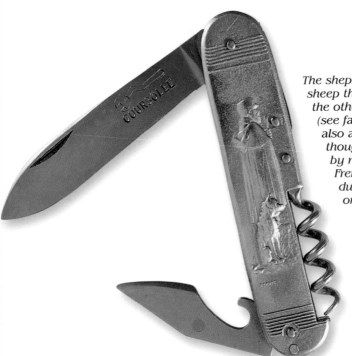

The shepherd is guarding sheep that are depicted on the other side of the knife (see facing page). It is also a Coursolle knife, though Coursolle was by no means the only French maker to reproduce country scenes on its coverings.

This is the reverse side of the Coursolle knife shown opposite. It contains a can-opener, a bottle-opener, a corkscrew, and a steel blade. The coverings are of brass.

This model shows a female basketball or netball player about to shoot. The other side depicts a male gymnast on the fixed bar. There is just one blade of thin steel, marked LD, and the fob ring is made of brass. Although it may be a Coursolle knife, the characteristic bands at the top and bottom of the coverings are incised rather than embossed, and there are fewer of them than on a typical Coursolle.

The boy who is annoying a sleeping dog is being bitten on the reverse covering. Although the style is very similar to that of a Coursolle, the knife is marked Pradel, another leading Thiers manufacturer. In any case, the name "Coursolle" came to describe a particular design of pocket knife and fell into the public domain. The coverings are of brass and it has six attachments, two of them blades.

The firm of Treille-Sugier, successor to the firm of Bellet & Treille of Thiers, produced this six-piece pocket knife, whose celluloid coverings depict a sporting theme. This one shows young people running a cross-country race.

These two Coursolle knives take Brittany as their theme. The one on the left shows a fisherman with his basket on one side and a view of a port on the other. The second knife depicts a bagpipe player on one side, and on the other a Breton wife scanning the horizon, a piece of embroidery on her lap.

These three automobile pocket knives are of very different origins. The top one is made by Taylor Cutlery of Kingsport, Tennessee; the center knife is a genuine French Coursolle dating from the 1920s, and the bottom one is a Coursolle-style knife, made in Taiwan.

France made an alliance with Russia during the First World War. This rather worn little pocket knife commemorates the event. On the one side, there is a French soldier holding a bugle, and on the other, a Russian soldier standing at ease with his weapon. Above the fighters are the inscriptions "France et Russie," and at their feet "vive l'armée" (long live the army).

Since even small knives were destined mainly for use by men, they were often decorated with female subjects considered risqué at the time. These rather charming examples are two sides of the same model of knife, made in Thiers in the 1930s.

*Men's
pastimes and interests
are often depicted on handle coverings, whether
drawn, engraved, hammered, or stamped. Dogs
feature commonly; women—of the respectable
kind—fairly rarely!*

These two handsome, limited edition knives have modern coverings of scrimshaw on bone. The knives are made by Kershaw, an American manufacturer. The engravings are by Walter Stefander. The engraving of the African elephant is marked 10 and dates from 1992, and the rhinoceros is numbered 12.

A French artist has
engraved the ivory covering
of this German Puma knife with the head of a
wild boar that has fearsome tusks.

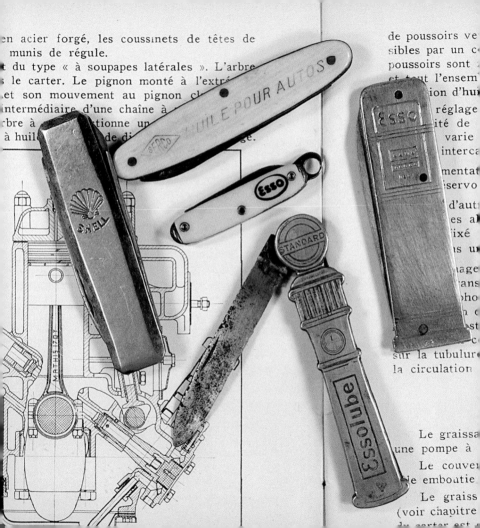

VI

PROMOTIONAL
pocket knives

A s the pocket companion *par excellence* and one that is of necessity inexpensive, the clasp-knife has given makers of promotional items plenty of ideas for publicity, starting from the dawn of the twentieth century, and continuing right up to the present day.

It is exciting to be given an attractive little two-bladed knife extolling the virtues of an aperitif, a make of champagne or a brand of gasoline. Millions of these gifts have survived, though many are badly worn through years of rubbing against small change in the pocket. For the collector, these modest items are often not worth much in monetary terms, but their sentimental value is great.

A set of Victorinox promotional gifts in their original boxes. From left to right are the Huntsman, the Mountaineer, and the Handyman, the latter having 14 attachments. On the facing page, from the bottom up, are the Spartan, the Compact, engraved with the logo of the Swiss post office, and the Explorer.

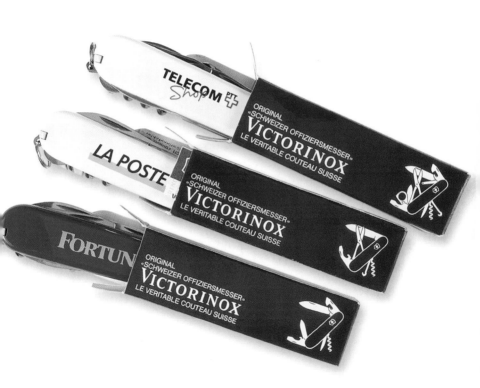

Many of these little promotional knives for a particular brand or tourist attraction are made to look like Victorinox Swiss army knives. In fact, they are but pale imitations, most of them from ...

... China. They are badly finished, and the blades are made of steel that is too soft for cutting, but they are to be found in large numbers all over the world. Beware of these imitations.

The top model is in
Solingen style and contains
a blade and a bottle-opener. It
was made to promote the French
photographic papers made by
Guilleminot. The bottom knife looks very much
like it but was actually made in Germany. It has
iridescent plastic coverings.

As in the two pocket knives
on the facing page, the blade is
here really just an accessory,
because the true purpose of this tool is
to open beer bottles.

This is a collection of pocket knives and bottle-openers of various makes, that were all promotional gifts for the Mumm brand of champagne. Yet it is well known that the bottles of this drink of kings are never opened with a corkscrew!

In the 1930s, little pocket knives were made in Thiers to promote the French Communist Party. The Socialist Party also had its own promotional knives.

Thiers was responsible for producing a great many of the thousands of French promotional knives that were very much in fashion between the wars and right through to the 1950s. They were made entirely of steel, like those on the facing page, or of steel covered with celluloid. They were of good quality, worthy representatives of some leading brands.

These types of pocket knife are different from those on the preceding pages. They were very practical because they are so flat, and they fitted neatly into the small vest pocket of café waiters, who wore a slightly shiny black vest over a large, white apron. The knife in the center, marked Cordon Rouge, a brand of Mumm champagne, has mother-of-pearl coverings. The knife on this page inscribed "Charles Heidsieck" (another brand of champagne) has an elegant mechanism for its corkscrew attachment.

Two sides of a promotional knife for Benedictine liqueur, made at Fécamp in Normandy. The coverings are of stamped nickel silver, decorated with two different designs. The blades are of steel. The knife dates from the 1920s. The technique of using stamped metal coverings was very popular in the late nineteenth century, especially in Germany.

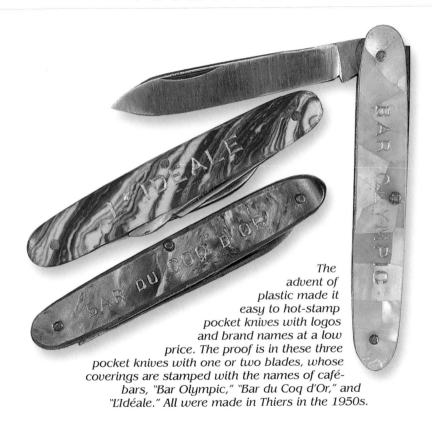

The advent of plastic made it easy to hot-stamp pocket knives with logos and brand names at a low price. The proof is in these three pocket knives with one or two blades, whose coverings are stamped with the names of café-bars, "Bar Olympic," "Bar du Coq d'Or," and "L'Idéale." All were made in Thiers in the 1950s.

The short, curved blade on this knife has a single purpose, namely to prepare for popping the cork on a bottle of champagne. The blade was used to remove the tin foil covering the whole bottle-top, then to ease away the metal wire holding the cork in place.

*This is a more elaborate
French knife, presented to good customers of Peugeot cycles,
whose factory is at Valentigney, near the Swiss border. The nickel silver linings are stamped with the trademark. There are two
blades and a screwdriver with a notch in the side that might
have been used for tightening the spokes in a bicycle wheel.*

The Germans favored coverings of stamped nickel silver. The two promotional knives above are for Vichy Délice and Vichy Quina, both types of liqueur. The one on the left, made in Solingen, is a commemorative knife for the Republic of Argentina.

Makers of champagne were particularly fond of promoting their brands by means of these little pocket knives with one or two blades and imitation ivory coverings. They first appeared in the early twentieth century and were still being manufactured in the 1950s. There is an intruder among them, a small Italian knife marked "L. Biasioli" of Genoa, promoting a meat extract!

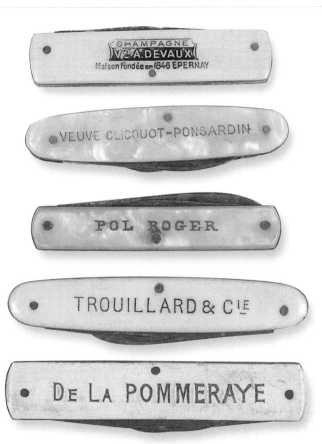

Index, Bibliography & Addresses

Index

The index includes the names of the most important manufacturers and places mentioned in the book.

Bibliography

J.B. Himsworth, *The Story of Cutlery, from Flint to Stainless Steel*. London: Ernest Benn Ltd., 1953.

Bernard Levine, *Levine's Guide to Pocket Knife Values*. Iola, WI: Krause Publ., 2000.

Bernard Levine, *Pocket Knives*. Edison, NJ: Chartwell Books Inc., 1998.

R. Stewart and R. Ritchie, *The Big Book of Pocket Knives*. Paducah, NY: Collector Books, 2000.

Bill Schweder, *Pocket Knives*. Paducah, NY: Collector Books (date unknown).

P. Smithurst, *The Cutlery Industry*. Princes Risborough: Shire Books, 1987.

Special acknowledgement is due to Camille Pagé, who between 1896 and 1904 compiled with diligence, conscientiousness, and intelligence a six-volume, 1,600-page history of cutlery, entitled *La Coutellerie des origines à nos jours* [Cutlery from its origins to the present day], a unique record of the craft that became an industry.

Addresses

United States

Knifemaker's Guild
PO Box 1019
Madisonville, TN 37354-1019
Tel: 423-442-5767

National Knife Collector's Association
PO Box 21070
Chattanooga, TN 37424-0070
Tel: 800-548-3907

United Kingdom

City Museum
Weston Park
Sheffield S10 2TP
Tel: 0114 278 2600
(currently closed for renovation)

Daniel Bexfield Antiques
26, Burlington Avenue
London W1V 9AD
Tel: 0207 491 1720
www.bexfield.co.uk

France

Musée le Secq des Tournelles
Rue Jacques Villon
76000 Rouen
Tel: 02 35 71 28 40

Thiers Cutlery Museum
58, rue de la Coutellerie
63300 Thiers
Tel: 04 73 80 58 86

Acknowledgments

This book would not have been possible without the valuable assistance of several people, and especially the following:

Mme Brigitte Liabeuf, Curator of the Musée de la Coutellerie de Thiers; Mme May Kindal, José Martins and Hélène Montsallier; M. Pierre Courty; M. and Mme Jean-Pierre Treille; M. Claude Geoffroy; Mme Vilma Laroche; M. Laurent Oiffer; Mme Marie Pessiot, Curator, Musée Le Secq des Tournelles, Rouen; Mrs Daniel Lerasle, Gilles Cotten, Francis Chabeaud, and Daniel Jallageas, collectors.

The translator would like to acknowledge the valuable assistance of Joan Unwin and Ken Hawley of the Hawley Collection, and Miss Oversby, all of Sheffield, UK.

Photographic credits:
All photographs are by Dominique Pascal and Antoine Pascal
and are taken from: Archives & Collections
e-mail: archives.collections@wanadoo.fr

In the same series

Collectible
CORKSCREWS
by Frédérique Crestin-Billet

FA0550-01-II
Dépôt légal: 04/2001